JOSE, CAN YOU SEE?

Jimmy Lumpkin

PublishAmerica
Baltimore

ISBN: 1-59129-326-X
PUBLISHED BY
PUBLISHAMERICA BOOK PUBLISHERS
www.publishamerica.com
Baltimore

Printed in the United States of America

This book is dedicated to my wife,

Betty Lumpkin.

Chapter I
THE QUESTION MARK IN THE SKY

At midnight I could still see the tower clearly outlined with lights against the dark sky. It was the first thing I saw every morning and the last thing I saw before going to sleep. That was because my bedroom window faced north toward the refinery, a half-mile from our house. I couldn't see the storage tanks because the trees hid them. But the black tower with a crook on top was taller than anything in Oak Grove.

"What's it for?" I once asked my father.

"I don't know its purpose," he said. "It's just there."

When I was little, I imagined the crooked tower to be a hay hook, like the one my uncle in Mexico used to lift bales of hay into his wagon. But now that I was twelve, I saw it as a question mark.

Some mornings I made up a sentence for it. "What will you do today, Jose?" or "Will I get an

'A' on the math test?" But mostly things just happened, and life made its own questions.

That summer of 1941, most of the people in our country talked about the war in Europe. They asked, "Will the United States fight, too?"

President Roosevelt said no. But many believed that, if Hitler wasn't stopped, Germany would take over the whole world. It had already captured France and some other countries.

The people of our town asked a second question. "Will there be a strike?"

Most of Oak Grove was connected with the oil refinery one way or another. Many of the workers felt they should be paid more money, but not all of them wanted to strike. Papá said it would be a bad thing. "Una huelga," as he called it, "would make trouble between the men who stop working and those who continue doing their jobs."

This strike talk caused much worry for my family. It was the reason I stayed awake past midnight that hot night in August. When Papá came home from the swing shift, I heard Mamá go into the kitchen to make him a snack. The smell of coffee drifted into my bedroom along with their conversation.

"Jose, (that's Papá's name, too) will you walk

out if the others do?"

"No, mi amor," he said. "For eight years, I've had a good job with the refinery. I will not go against it now."

"But the strikers. They sometimes do bad things to workers who refuse to join them."

It sounded as if Mamá had hiccups, but I knew that she was crying. Papá's chair scraped against the floor as he went over to console her.

A little while later he came into my room to tuck me in. He still did that even though I wasn't a little boy anymore. Only this time I stood at the window looking at the crooked tower.

"What do you see out there?" he asked.

"Just the question mark, Papá. Only tonight it looks like an evil serpent standing on its tail. Hear it hissing?"

"It's just the steam, Mijo."

That was his work at the refinery – making steam. He was a boiler fireman. I had seen the boilers many times when I carried dinner to my father. There were four of the big rusty things that looked like locomotives without wheels. They made the steam which passed through pipes and worked the pumps. "Swish, swish," said these machines as they pushed the oil through the lines to the tank cars waiting on the railroad track.

I crawled back into bed, and he kissed me good night. I could still smell the oil on his clothing after he left. "Smells like money," Papá used to joke. But that was before the strike talks started earlier this summer. Smells like trouble, I thought.

It was hot. Much too hot for sleep. For a long time I just lay there sweating and remembering.

When we moved to Texas from Mexico I was only four years old. We came here to pick cotton. Every morning before daylight the trucks picked us up at the campground and carried us to the fields. It was cool at that hour and damp. As the sun climbed above the trees along the fence row, the dew on the cotton leaves sparkled like tiny diamonds. Then it got hot. Really hot.

Stooped over like animals walking on four legs, the workers scrambled between the rows of plants. Their hands moved so fast you could hardly see them. They snatched the white, fluffy cotton from each green plant and dropped it into the long bags the pickers pulled behind them.

My whole family did that, even Mamá who was very big with Marikita. I crawled along beside her, putting what little cotton I gathered into her bag.

Later I became "water boy" and struggled across the rows with the bucket when someone called, "Agua." There were two long-handled, enamel dippers inside the water bucket for drinking. I was always happy when a worker dumped one of them on his head to cool off. With a lighter load, I moved on the to next thirsty cotton picker.

Finally the sun went down, and the trucks hauled us back to camp. After our supper of frijoles and tortillas, cooked outside on a wood fire, we bathed in the river. Then we slept in the open because the tents were too hot.

I remember how hard the ground felt, even though we spread our quilts on the grass. For a long time I lay there staring up into the mossy oaks. The trees reminded me of old, bearded men standing guard over us so that we wouldn't run away. Finally sleep came, then morning and the cotton fields all over again.

For us, that ended when Papá got a good job at the refinery. Only lately it hadn't been so good. Something bad is going to happen there, I thought.

When I finally fell asleep, I had that nightmare again, the one about when I had been in first grade. I didn't know much English then.

Once, while the other kids were singing, "Oh say can you see," I sang, "Jose, can you see." Miss Branson thought I had changed the words on purpose and scolded me in front of the whole class.

Since then every time I went to bed nervous or upset, I had that bad dream.

The next time I looked out my window, the sky had turned pink. Jose, can you see by the dawn's early light? I thought.

Yes, already I see the question mark clearly. I made a sentence for it. Will something bad happen to Papá if there's a strike?

Chapter II
HOW FAR CAN YOU SPIT?

I awoke a second time that morning to the sound of giggling. At first I thought I was having another nightmare. But it was just Marikita, my little sister. She peeked at me through the half-open door. Her freckled face twisted into a grin as she asked, "How far can you spit?"

Getting up on one elbow, I threw my pillow at her. She slammed the door in time to stop it. I could still hear her giggling as she raced down the hall.

Since I was the only boy, I had a room to myself, and my three sisters shared one. That made them jealous, so they always pestered me.

A little while after Marikita left, Mamá knocked and opened the door. "Desayuno," she called cheerfully. Breakfast was ready. The hot, spicy aroma of chorizo drifted in with the smell of fresh coffee.

Slipping into some jeans and pulling the t-shirt over my head couldn't have taken long. But when I strolled into the kitchen, Mamá, Papá, Violeta, Rosita, and Marikita were already sitting around the big, wooden table. As I sat down, they stared at me like I was wearing curlers. Then I remembered.

"Excuse me!" I said, jumping up. Rushing to the hall mirror, I ran a pocket comb through my black, wavy hair. In the Díaz family, nobody was permitted to the table with uncombed hair. "That's as bad as unwashed hands," Papá said.

Another custom was praying, so, like always, we joined hands and took turns thanking God for some special blessing. Papá praised God for giving him a good job. Mamá thanked Him for our food. The twins mentioned their quinceañera, or fifteenth birthday celebration, coming in November. I told God how glad I was to have a special friend. And Marikita said, "Thank you for letting me spit so far," then excused herself to go to the bathroom.

"What's this thing about Marikita spitting?" Papá asked, starting the platter of huevos around the table.

Taking the eggs, I explained, "She's lost a front tooth and has learned to spit very well through the gap."

"I hope she grows another tooth soon," Mamá said, shaking her head.

My little sister returned to the table. Although she was four, she acted as though she'd forgotten how to eat. First, she dropped a tortilla. Next, a chorizo sausage bounced off her plate, hit the chair, then rolled under the table. Marikita scampered after it.

"Just sit on the floor," Papá said, "and we'll pass the food down to you."

Everyone laughed except Mamá who frowned.

Our conversation was scrambled like the eggs. Mamá asked Papá about getting a new pressure cooker, a machine used for canning fruits and vegetables. "The tomatoes are rotting in the garden because I have no way to preserve them."

Why didn't he just say, "Okay, buy one"? But Papá twisted his mustache, like he always did before making a major decision. Then, with a stern expression on his face, he said, "No, I need a new set of golf clubs more."

Mamá smiled. Papá didn't play golf, but he liked to tease.

The señoritas were always the same. Sitting there next to each other in their yellow and red dresses, they reminded me of a couple of parrots. They looked alike, dressed alike, and smelled alike, since they used the same perfume. They even talked the same. At breakfast they went on and on about their quinceañera.

Bored, I stared at the big, yellow sunflowers on the wall paper, then at the smaller ones on the table cloth.

My little sister mocked me. She looked up and down, then grinned at me with those dimpled cheeks. She reminded me of a sunflower, too, maybe because she was always so bright and cheerful.

Finally there came a gap in the conversation, like the one between Marikita's teeth. And through it I spit out the question I'd been holding for an hour. "Papá," I said, "Why don't you quit working at the refinery?"

Everyone stared at me as if I'd just said a bad word.

"I don't mean forever. Just until the trouble is over."

"And while we wait for that, where will we get money for the quinceañera or your school clothes? Were you thinking, perhaps, of picking cotton again?"

My face burned with embarrassment.

Just then a knock sounded. Marikita raced to

the door, her pigtails bouncing up and down like two little springs. When she opened it, I saw my friend, Owl, standing there.

"Hola, Ricardo," she said, grabbing his hand and leading him into the kitchen. "How far can you spit?"

If it'd been anyone else, I'd have died. But Owl was not just a friend. He was my very best friend.

I didn't know why. We were not at all alike. Richard Krause was chubby, fair-skinned and blue-eyed. He kept his blond hair cut in a flat top. His round face and thick-lensed glasses made him look like an owl. So that was what I called him. Owl. He was smart and knew how to talk German and English.

Me, I was just a slim, dark-skinned Mexican with sisters who drove me loco. But, thank goodness, Owl came often to take me away on some new adventure.

He gobbled down a couple of tortillas. "Ready?" he asked, looking at his watch as if he had an appointment.

"Sure," I said, getting up from the table.

"Te portas bien!" Mamá said.

She always told me to be good when I left with Owl. That was because we had this reputation. At school the teachers called us "the troublesome twosome." They wanted to separate us but couldn't, because we were in the same reading group.

Marikita followed us to the door. "Where you go?" she asked.

I ignored the question which didn't make sense and, anyway, wasn't any of her business. Pushing my bike out of the garage, I joined Owl at the front gate where he and my little sister were taking turns seeing how far they could spit. Marikita's floppy-eared hound came around the corner of the porch and stood in front of them, wagging his tail. "Get out of the way, Fleas, or I'll spit on you," Owl said.

Marikita put her hands on her hips and glared at Owl. "You not talk to my dog like that, Ricardo. His name is Feliz, not Fleas. Say Fe-liz."

"Fe-liz," Owl repeated, petting the hound.

Owl was a friend I didn't ever want to be without. Nothing will ever separate us, I thought as we rode off together on our bicycles.

Chapter III
WHOSE CHILD ARE YOU?

The gravel crunched under the balloon tires of our Western Flyers as we peddled along the narrow lane with the sun in our faces. Owl's bike was bright blue and mine a rusty red thing that had once been Violeta's.

The kids at school sometimes teased me about riding a girl's bicycle. "I like it," I told them, "because I can get on and off fast." But really I wished I had one like Owl's. Papá said he'd buy me a new one right after he got his golf clubs. I figured that was like waiting for a snail to crawl around the world.

"Where are we going?" I asked Owl, who took the lead.

"Follow me," he said.

At the main highway we turned north and rode along the shoulder into Oak Grove. When he crossed Main, Owl yelled, "Race you to the dam," and charged up the sidewalk as if he'd just seen a ghost.

I flew up the other side, the one that went past the stores. I caught a glimpse of some customers inside Woolworth's, their mouths open in surprise as I sped by. But the real problem came when Mrs. Peabody stepped through the door of Piggly Wiggly with a sack of groceries in her arms. I missed her, but she screamed and scattered cans everywhere.

While I looked back at her, Sheriff Madfellow came out of the barber shop to see what all the commotion was about. I tried to swerve. But he stepped right in front of my bike. SMACK! He staggered back into the red-and-white barber pole, which tipped over and rolled into the street.

I lay on the sidewalk, hoping I was dead.

Jerking me up, the sheriff dangled me in front of him like I was a muñeco, a puppet. His face twisted in anger. I smelled the tobacco juice which looked like brown worms crawling down each side of his mouth. His eyes burned right through me. He spoke slowly, as though I didn't understand English. "Whose child are you?" he asked.

I shook all over and so did my voice. "Jose Díaz, Sir."

"Oh, that refinery Mex. I'm going to have a talk with him. And you! If you ever ride on the sidewalk again…"

"No, Sir," I said, shaking my head. "I won't."

When he put me down, I grabbed my bicycle and pushed it across the street to where Owl stood beside his, looking as innocent as an angel. "Whose child are you?" he asked, grinning.

With the sun warm on our backs, we rode to the west edge of town, past the cotton gin which roared with the sound of many machines all going at once. Some trucks lined up at the scales while others waited to be unloaded at a tin building. There a gin worker stood on a load of cotton, swinging the big, metal spout back and forth. This sucked the fluffy, white cotton into the gin which removed the seeds.

After crossing the long, concrete bridge over the Río Frío, we left the highway and followed a dirt road into the park. A large banner hanging between two trees said, "WELCOME COTTON PICKERS."

I hoped that we wouldn't see any of them. Cotton picking was a part of my past I wanted to forget. I was relieved to find the camp empty except for a couple of old men, sitting in front of their tents.

"What's it like picking cotton?" Owl asked as we rode beneath the oaks all bearded with moss.

"How should I know?"

His eyes opened wide. "My dad said your family used to be migrant workers."

"That was a long time ago," I said.

My mind drifted back to those unpleasant days. "River Rats." That's what people called us because we lived in a filthy place by the river. There weren't any toilets. We just went behind the bushes. A bad stench always hung over camp.

"River sure is low," I said, hoping to change the subject. Some kids were walking across the dam with the green water just hiding their ankles.

We rode to our special place where the willows stretched their long arms over the river. A rope dangled from one of these branches. Before I could even stop, Owl piled off his bike. Charging down the river bank, he grabbed the rope and swung out over the water while beating his chest with one hand and yelling like Tarzan. Letting go, he dropped fully clothed into the middle of the stream. "Come on in!" he shouted. "The water's fine."

"You're loco!" I said. But, after taking off my shoes and shirt, I caught the swing and jumped in, too.

A bunch of little kids were wading next to the dam with their mothers watching. One little boy called to me in Spanish, "How deep is the water over there?"

But I just shook my head like I didn't understand.

For a long time Owl and I played there in the shade. Sometimes we swam on our backs in the cool water, spouting like whales. Then we got out and jumped off the swing again.

I wished that summer would never end and that Owl and I would always be together, doing whatever we wanted to do whenever we wanted to do it.

But even from the river I spotted that question mark tower through a gap in the trees. And I heard the steam pumps at the refinery swishing back and forth. They seemed to say, "Whose child are you? Whose child are you?"

I thought of Papá. Even though he liked to joke, he was very strict, especially with me, his only son. "If you wear my name," he told me, "you have to take care of it."

I knew that I would be punished when Papá found out about my running into the sheriff. I just didn't know how.

Maybe he won't let me run around with Owl anymore, I thought.

Chapter IV
WHOSE JOB ARE YOU?

I didn't see Owl the next day because of the pig. Papá brought him home from town early that morning, and it was his squealing that woke me up. At first I thought it was Marikita who sometimes made a noise like that to get my attention.

Dressing quickly, I rushed from room to room. No one was in the house except me. I heard that squeal again and Feliz's barking coming from somewhere outside.

Opening the back door, I saw Mamá, the twins, and Marikita standing by the barn. I thought the hound had found another rattler, and the squealing was coming from the girls.

Racing out to see the snake, I scattered squawking hens in every direction.

"Jose, por favor," scolded Mamá with her hands on her hips.

"Sorry, Mamá," I said, slowing to a walk.

Papá had rented five acres of land on the edge

of Oak Grove so we could raise animals. Most important of all were these chickens because they provided the eggs Mamá traded for groceries.

Taking care of the hundred or so Rhode Island Reds was the twins' job. Every morning the señoritas tossed a couple of buckets of grain on the ground for the chickens to eat and filled their trough with water. Late every afternoon the girls went into the hen house to gather eggs.

Papá had made the chickens' nests from apple crates and lined them with cloth sacks so that the eggs wouldn't get broken. He'd placed the boxes on shelves along each wall of the tin building. The nests were high enough that snakes weren't supposed to get into them. Only sometimes they did. That was why I liked watching my big sisters collect eggs.

Violeta or Rosita would move slowly along each wall, putting the eggs carefully into their straw baskets. But if either twin found one of the black chicken snakes in a nest, they'd both jump up and down screaming much louder than a squealing pig and scattering eggs all over the chicken house. Seeing them do that snake dance was more fun for me than going to the Saturday matinee at the Rialto theater.

Both Mamá and Papá took care of our brown cow, Jersey, and her baby calf, Buttermilk. Papá milked Jersey every morning and Mamá did it in the evening after he'd gone to work. They fed her from the bales of hay stacked along the back wall of the barn.

Now there was a new animal to take care of. We all stared at the little, pink critter in Papá's hands. The pig stopped squealing when he put it down on the barn floor. The newcomer made little grunting noises as Feliz sniffed at it. "What do you think of him?" Marikita asked her dog.

Last December my little sister wanted a puppy for Navidad – Christmas. Papá said, "No! We only raise useful animals. You can't eat or milk a dog. Besides, they break eggs and kill chickens."

Marikita was very sad.

What happened Christmas morning was hard for any of us to believe. Mamá read the story about Baby Jesus being born in a manger "What's a manger?" asked Marikita.

"It's a barn where animals are kept," Mamá said.

So Marikita ran to look inside ours. I didn't know what she expected to find, but a stray hound was there, sleeping in the hay. Marikita ran back to the house. "Come see my dog," she said.

At first we didn't believe there really was one, not until we went to the barn with Marikita and saw it. "His name is Feliz Navidog," she said, "but you can just call him Feliz."

On hearing his name, the hound raised his floppy ears from the hay and looked at her with those sad eyes. Papá didn't have the heart to get rid of him, especially since Marikita said God gave Feliz to her for a Christmas present. "Since God gave you this beast, Marikita, you must take care of him," Papá said.

And she did, feeding him scraps from the table and keeping his dish filled with water.

Feliz was a good dog. Once he killed a rattlesnake in the hay, and many times he chased away coyotes and raccoons that were trying to get the chickens.

I used to take care of a little white chivo, a goat. He had long curved horns and loved to butt anything that moved. His life almost ended the day he knocked Mamá into a wash tub full of soapy water. Right after he ate the upholstery from our old Ford, the goat suddenly disappeared.

"Where is Billy Gruff?" Marikita asked at

dinner that night.

Everyone stared at Papá. "Billy is around here somewhere," he said, passing the barbecue to me. I felt a little guilty eating it, but not much. I didn't like taking care of animals.

Now there was this new pig. Reaching down and scratching him on the head, I asked, "Whose job are you?"

He just grunted, but everyone else pointed at me.

I looked at the twins, standing there grinning. "Maybe I could gather the eggs and you could…"

"No, no, no!" they said, shaking their finger at me.

I looked down at the pig. "Your name is Pork Chop."

I spent most of that day making him a pen between the barn and chicken house. First, I dug four holes in the ground with Papá's post hole digger. Next, I dropped in the mesquite posts and packed the dirt around them. Then I stretched chicken wire around the square and stapled it to the four posts. Last of all, I put inside two wooden troughs and the pig.

Every day I fed him corn and the extra milk left over from Jersey. Pork Chop was cute, but I didn't let myself grow very fond of him. Christmas was coming again in a few months.

Chapter V
WHAT'S YOUR NAME?

Papá didn't say anything about my getting into trouble with the sheriff. A week dragged by, then another. I did a lot of sweating and not just from the August heat. Each morning I looked out my window at the question mark in the sky and wondered, today will Papá find out that I've been bad?

Some days his face was stern and unsmiling, like the picture of George Washington hanging on the wall at school. Did he already know that I ran into the sheriff with my bicycle?

"Why does Papá seem angry?" I asked Mamá in the garden. "Is he mad with me about something?"

She just shrugged, then continued picking the red, ripe tomatoes, laying them gently into her straw basket.

One morning when I looked out my window at the question mark, I saw the answer. There stood my bicycle, chained to a post in the yard fence. Qué horrible! I thought. And this the first day of school!

Mamá handed me my sack lunch as I hurried out the door. I trotted to Owl's place which was right down the lane from ours.

He lived in a little, white house with a pointy, tin roof and a stove pipe sticking out the top. A lot of homes in the country around Oak Grove were like that. Even ours, until Papá added a front porch and Mamá filled it with potted flowers. I think all these houses were built by the same carpenter who had only one set of plans.

Owl sometimes waited for me out front under the big mesquite, but today the chair swing was empty. I didn't knock on the door because his folks weren't friendly. They always looked at me like I was trying to sell magazines or something. Then they said, "He's not here," or, "Wait in the yard."

I didn't see him there so I jogged toward the highway. But a little while later I heard the crunching of gravel and jumped out of the way as Owl shot past on his shiny, blue bicycle. Skidding to a stop, he grinned. "Don't tell me. A man with a mustache took your bike."

I nodded.

Climbing on those handlebars had to be the dumbest thing I've ever done. Owl hit every bump between his house and town just to hear me groan. Then he tried to run over any kid who happened to be walking close to the street. Someone threw an apple core which bounced off my shoulder.

Finally we stopped in front of the school. As Owl pushed his bike into the wooden rack next to a lot of others, a group of boys standing on the lawn called to him. "Hey, Rich, where you been all summer? Hanging out with that Mex?" They all laughed.

Ignoring the clowns, I limped up the sidewalk toward the brown, stucco buildings tied together with a string of corridors. Just as I reached our classroom, Norman bounced out the door clanging the long-handled bell. He was the tallest boy in school but acted like a little kid. Every year he persuaded the teacher to let him ring her bell.

Pausing at one of the darkened windows, I started to comb my hair. But Owl grabbed me by the elbow and pulled me inside.

There were two seventh grades, 7A and 7B. "A" was made up of the smart kids. "B" was for those of us a little slow in English or reading.

Owl could have made the "A" class except he wasn't "properly motivated." That was what our teacher told him last year.

We sat down together in the back row. Everything looked really clean, like it always did on the first day. The floor was spotless and smelled of new wax. All the books had been dusted and filed in the shelves along both walls. Our desks were in straight rows facing the front. Even the ink wells in them practically overflowed with black ink.

That reminded me of when we had been in fourth grade. Jo Ann sat in front of me with her pig tails dangling just above my desk. I pretended to dip one of them into the ink well. Then Owl reached over and really did it. We both got into trouble at school. But when Papá heard about it, he gave me swats at home. I didn't sit down for about a week.

I was pretty sure that we wouldn't do something like that in this class. Mrs. Dozier was big, not just tall but gorda – fat. And she looked mean. She stood there at the front of the classroom under the portrait of George Washington, the one where his teeth were hurting.

Maybe he's the patron saint of school

teachers, I thought. Mrs. Dozier didn't smile even once as she read our names from the attendance book in her huge hands.

We responded with "present" or "here," and everything went well until those two new kids walked in. He wore a tie, and she looked like she was going to a wedding. I figured they'd come straight from Mexico.

"What are your names?" asked Mrs. Dozier.

They just stood there by the door while the whole class stared at them. Then I opened my big mouth. "Digan sus nombres."

Like magic the boy snapped to attention. "Roberto García Morales, a sus órdenes," he said.

"María de Jesús González Rodríguez, a sus órdenes," the girl said, curtsying.

"Awaiting your orders" was a polite response in Latin America, but here in Texas it was only good for laughs. That wasn't what got me started, though. I didn't even grin when Mrs. Dozier said, "Ah, so you're brother and sister."

But when I looked at Owl, he rolled his eyes like a couple of pin balls. I giggled, then the whole class did.

"Stop that right now!" yelled the teacher.

Then, staring at me, she added, "You

apologize to those Órdenes children right now. Shame on you for laughing at them."

I turned to the new boy and girl who looked like they were about to cry. "Mrs. Dozier thinks your last name is 'Órdenes'," I explained in Spanish. "She has you down as brother and sister."

They looked at each other and giggled, which set off the whole class again. Mrs. Dozier glared at me, her hands on her hips. "What did you say to them? You were talking about me, weren't you?"

Norman looked up at the clock in front of the room and snatched the bell from her desk. I thought Mrs. Dozier was going to kill him when he rang it. But while she scolded him, I escaped. That's what it means to be saved by the bell, I thought, as the other students followed me out of home room.

Well, maybe 'saved' isn't the right word for it. I figured Mrs. Dozier would be waiting for me last period when I returned to her for math. I just hoped she didn't have George Washington's hatchet, the one he used to chop down the cherry tree.

Chapter VI
WHAT WILL YOU WRITE TONIGHT, JOSE?

Our next teacher, Miss Rose, stood in the doorway of her classroom, smiling and greeting us like we were special. Qué bonita! I thought. Her long, blue dress was the color of her eyes which sparkled as she said things such as "Welcome" and "Glad you're here."

Inside, the walls were covered with portraits of famous authors. I didn't know many of them, but I recognized Samuel Clemens by his long, gray hair and mustache.

Huck Finn and Tom Sawyer were my favorite characters. I guess that was because they always got into trouble like Owl and me. Sometimes when we played on the Río Frío, I pretended that it was the Mississippi River and that Owl and I were Huck and Tom.

I turned around to ask Owl where he wanted to sit. But he took a seat by some other boys near the front because the "órdenes" kids were following me to the back like a couple of puppies. If they thought we were going to be friends just because we were Mexicans, they could swim back across the Río Grande.

I sat down, trapped by Roberto on one side and María on the other. She'd either put on too much perfume or had fallen into a honeysuckle vine. I thought, what a fun day this is going to be!

The only thing right about it was Miss Rose. Most teachers hide their first name like some deep secret. But she talked to us like we were real people. "My name is Sharon Rose," she said, "and I'm happy to be your teacher for the language arts block."

She explained that language arts included English grammar, literature, vocabulary, and composition.

Everything had a different name in junior high. Literature used to be just reading. Vocabulary included spelling, but we also had to know the meaning of the words. "Grammar is how the language is built," Miss Rose said.

Today we took turns diagraming sentences on the board. I wasn't very good at it, so the teacher gave me an easy one. When I finished, it looked like this: The boy (subject) hit (simple predicate) the ball (direct object).

Some kids clapped for me but not Owl. "BORING," he said, rolling his eyes. The boys sitting next to him laughed, and I felt my face burning with embarrassment as I sat back down.

I thought grammar was interesting, like putting together pieces of a puzzle.

But even better was the poem called Paul Revere's Ride by Henry Wadsworth Longfellow. Miss Rose divided the class up and had each group read a section of the poem out loud. "Choral reading," it was called. You could almost hear the horse's hoof beats.

Just before lunch time our teacher gave us our composition assignment. "I want each of you to buy a notebook and write in it every day," she said.

"Write what?" Gerald asked, wiggling his freckled nose like there was a fly on it.

"Anything," she said, pacing back and forth at the front of the classroom. Her long, blond hair hung down her back like yellow twine, and reminded me of Rapunzel in the fairy tale. "Write what interests you," she said. "Things that you did or want to do. Tell about sports, your family, friends, school, the good times you've had, and the bad. Write about things that are important in your life."

"Oh, so it's like a diary," said Margaret. She pulled a pencil out of her purse, ready to get started.

"That's just the first part of the assignment," said Miss Rose. "The second part is to rewrite your experiences along a common subject, or theme. In fact, that's what we call it – a theme."

"I don't know how," drawled Ralph, making the four words sound like forty. Everyone laughed at the tall red-head sitting on the front row who always responded that way to anything he didn't want to do.

"I'll help you with that later," said Miss Rose. "But for now just do a page or two in your notebook every night. About the first of December you'll begin organizing your journals into themes. They're due just before Christmas vacation. That'll give me time to grade your wonderful stories."

Several kids groaned and others giggled.

"Your marks will be based on how well you follow the grammar rules we learn in class and on good spelling and punctuation. But most important of all, MAKE SENSE! If I can't understand your theme, you'll get an 'F'. And that doesn't mean 'fantastic'."

We all laughed.

I already knew what I'd write about — my family and my best friend, Owl. Only I wasn't certain about where to start. I finally decided that earlier in the summer would be a good place because that was when the trouble at the refinery began. Also, I could tell about the adventures that Owl and I had during vacation.

When someone in Mrs. Dozier's room stepped outside and clanged the bell, everyone jumped up. "Jose, could I see you a minute?" asked Miss Rose.

I waited by her desk while the other kids filed out to lunch. "Would you explain the writing assignment to Roberto and Maria? I want them to be part of this class, too."

"Okay, but they only know how to write in Spanish."

She nodded. "Maybe I could hire you to translate?"

"I'll do it for free," I said, starting for the door. Then, stopping, I asked her about where to start my theme. "Teacher, is it all right if I tell about some things that have already happened?"

She smiled. "Of course, Jose. Our past helps determine what we are and what we will be."

"Someday I'll be a writer," I said, hoping she wouldn't laugh.

Instead, she said, "I'm glad to hear that, Jose, and if you need help with this assignment, please call on me."

Stepping outside, I spotted the question mark towering above all the trees and houses of Oak Grove. I made a sentence for it: What will you write tonight, Jose?

Chapter VII
HOW CAN I ADD FRIENDS
WITHOUT SUBTRACTING?

I took my sack lunch to one of the little round tables in the patio and sat down to wait for Owl. He brought his tray out of the cafeteria and started to join me. But when he saw the "órdenes" kids coming, he hurried over to some boys sitting at the long wooden table under the live oak.

I started to move there, too, but they suddenly spread out. "It's already too crowded here," said Rex.

"All right, T-Rex." I called him that because he was as big as a dinosaur. Being the Baptist preacher's son, he liked to show off.

"What do y'all think of Miss Rose?" he asked. "Ain't she a good-looker?"

The other boys laughed and nodded like pecking hens. T-Rex liked to be funny, only he wasn't.

Roberto and María just stood there, staring at me like I was a movie star or something. "Go somewhere else," I told them in English.

I guess they took that as an invitation because they sat down beside me. I didn't feel like eating anymore, so, with a long toss, landed my sandwich in the trash can. The órdenes kids laughed and clapped. I guess they thought I was playing basket lunch.

Each of them pushed one of their tacos to me on a napkin. The carne asada, or broiled beef, smelled so good I couldn't help eating with the new boy and girl while they told me a really sad story. They weren't Mexicans, like I'd thought, but cousins from El Salvador. Their families had come here to escape the fighting in that country.

"Con permiso," Roberto said as the two stood up. "We have to go to the office of the nurse now and get some shots."

How polite, I thought, asking permission before leaving.

The boys at the long table didn't, though. They giggled and mocked us for speaking Spanish. "I don't like any of you," I said, my voice cracking.

All of them laughed harder except for Owl. He started to get up but T-Rex grabbed his arm.

"You don't need that Mex."

With a lump in my throat, I strolled over and plopped down on the lawn by the social studies room. A little while later I heard a rustling noise and looked up as a ton of grass dropped on my face. Through blurry eyes I saw Owl standing above me. "Avalanche," he said, grinning like we were friends again.

I started to chase him when Norman began clanging the school bell. After Owl helped me brush the junk out of my hair, we charged inside to claim our seats in the back of the room.

All of the bulletin boards were covered with history stuff. A large world map filled one wall. Red arrows went out from Germany to the countries it had already defeated such as Poland and France. Now Hitler's Nazis were fighting Britain and Russia.

A thin man with gray hair stood at the front of the classroom. "My name is Mr. Bradshaw," he said. "This is social studies which means geography and history. Most of the time we'll be studying about the war."

He moved over to a map of the Far East. "Who can tell me about the Triple Alliance?"

None of us knew anything about that so Mr. Bradshaw answered his own question. "Last year

Japan entered into that treaty with Germany and Italy. War against any one of those countries means war against all of them."

I raised my hand. "Mr. Bradshaw, will the United States get into the war?"

He nodded. "Soon as she gets a chance, Japan will attack the U.S.A. Then we'll be fighting against Japan, Italy, and Germany."

I figured that he was just guessing because I heard President Roosevelt say on the radio that the United States would stay out of the war being fought in Asia and Europe.

When the bell rang, I became worried about the war Mrs. Dozier and I had in homeroom that morning. I guess she must have forgotten about it, though. When 7-B went back to her the last period for math, she gave us some times and division problems to work from the board. I was the first one to turn in the paper. Mrs. Dozier checked it while I waited at her desk. Then, smiling for the first time that day, she announced to the whole class, "Jose got one hundred percent."

That made me feel good. But, best of all, Owl was with me again, like nothing had happened between us. Then María and Roberto came in late and sat down by us.

Frowning, Owl moved into an empty seat up front.

All around me students were copying the equations from the board, then working them on their paper. Some kids were even counting on their fingers because they didn't know their multiplication tables. How easy this is, I thought, but not my problem.

I tried to figure it out. I can have two new friends, or I can keep my best friend, Owl. I looked at him sitting there in the front row.

I can't give him up, I decided. We've always been there for each other and done things together. Only now Owl thinks I'm letting someone else take his place. Well, I'm not going to do that.

When we were dismissed, the two kids from El Salvador followed me outside. Before I could tell them to leave me alone, María hugged me and Roberto shook my hand. "Hasta mañana!" they said. "Until tomorrow."

"Come on," Owl said, jerking his bicycle from the rack.

I climbed on the handlebars, and he peddled us quickly down the street.

"Do you remember how lost I felt when I first came here from Mexico?" I asked.

"So?"

"Then you became my friend, and I owned the world."

"So?"

I looked back at María and Roberto still standing in front of the school, waving. "So they need friends, too."

For a long time we rode in silence. Then Owl said, "'Amigo.' That's how you say it. Right?"

"Sí, 'amigo'."

From his answer I thought I was going to have three friends. But towering above the trees and the houses stood my question mark. Can I really add two friends without subtracting one?

Chapter VIII
WHERE ARE ROBERTO AND MARÍA?

The next morning I looked out my window at the question mark in the sky and wondered, where's my bicycle? It wasn't chained to the fence. Did Papá sell it?

Slipping into my jeans and t-shirt, I ran barefooted into the garage and found it leaning against the wall beside our Model A Ford.

When I came out, I saw my father standing in the doorway of the house, twisting his mustache. I ran up and hugged him. "Thank you, Papá."

"Te portas bien, Mijo."

"I'll be good," I said, and even remembered to comb my hair at the hall mirror before joining the rest of the family for breakfast.

We had barely finished our prayer when Owl knocked. Papá sighed, and Marikita, like always, swung open the door. "Hola, Ricardo," she greeted Owl, then led him to the table where he gulped down a couple of tortillas. "Ready?" he asked, looking at his watch.

The sun climbed above the trees as we rode our bicycles up the gravel lane to the highway and followed it a half-mile into town. This time we arrived at school early. But already Roberto and María were there, waiting for us at the bicycle rack. "Buenos días," they greeted us.

"Good morning," both Owl and I answered. Then he added, "Me llamo Ricardo," like Marikita had taught him to say his name. He shook hands with Roberto first, then with María.

Both kids looked surprised but told Owl that they were pleased to meet him. He tried to be their friend, but at school that wasn't easy.

In language arts I explained a writing assignment to Roberto and María. They'd do it in Spanish, then I would translate it into English for Miss Rose. Only Mr. Tuffit, the principal, walked in while I was talking to them. Frowning, he shouted, "We have a rule against speaking Spanish on campus!"

The teacher's face turned red. "How can these two new kids from El Salvador do their assignment unless someone gives it to them in the only language they understand?"

He shrugged. "They'll just have to learn English."

It must have been embarrassing to Owl,

eating with us at lunch time while I whispered things to the new kids in Spanish. He kept looking around to see if Mr. Tuffit or any of the teachers were watching.

The next day that problem disappeared. After Owl and I parked our bikes, I looked around for Roberto and María. Instead of finding them, I spotted T-Rex waddling toward us.

He grinned as if he'd just layed an egg. "Hey, Jose, can you see? Your new friends, that is. They're not here."

"What do you mean?" I asked.

"Haven't you heard? The Border Patrol raided the cotton camp last night. The river rats are all gone, even that cute María."

I felt my face burning like a coal of fire. Doubling up my fists, I was about to pound the dinosaur when Owl grabbed my arm.

"Let it go!" he said.

I didn't back off, though, and neither did T-Rex. We stood there by the bike rack glaring at each other until Norman stepped out of Mrs. Dozier's room clanging her bell.

In homeroom, everyone was talking about the Border Patrol raid on the migrant workers camp. Even Gerald, who was usually very nice, said, "They loaded those greasers on a bus and shipped them back to Mexico where they belong."

"That's enough of that kind of talk," said Mrs. Dozier. "They're not 'greasers'. Besides," she added, glancing first at Juanita, then at me, "We have two of the cleanest Mexicans in the world right here in our class."

Several of the children clapped, but I felt really embarrassed. I think Juanita did, too, because she slid down in her seat and hid her face behind the big, red dictionary on her desk.

Owl sat by me in all of our classes, but he didn't say much. He always knew when I was sad.

After school we rode our bicycles slowly through town. As we passed the cotton gin, I noticed that no trucks were lined up to unload. Bales of cotton were stacked tall as the tin building, but the machinery inside was silent

The park on the Río Frío was quiet, too. Only a little water flowed over the dam. Long strands of Spanish moss dangled from the live oaks over the empty migrant workers' camp. Pieces of clothing lay scattered here and there along with cans and bottles. The WELCOME COTTON PICKERS banner had been torn down and lay in some weeds.

"So much for the welcome," I said, pumping back up the hill to the highway.

"Don't take it so hard," Owl said. "You still have me as a friend."

"Thanks."

Even though I was glad to have Owl as my best friend, I couldn't sleep that night, thinking about Roberto and María. I'd known them only two days, but they'd treated me really special. I felt badly that I'd been mean to them at first, wishing they'd go away. Now that they were gone, I wanted them back. Sitting there on my bed, I stared out the window at the question mark in the sky.

Why? Why? Why? hissed the steam pumps.

A little after twelve, Papá came into my room to kiss me good night. "Why did la migra raid the camp?" I asked him.

For a long time he, too, looked at the refinery. I knew that his mind was stringing words together so he could answer me in English. "It's fall," he said, running his fingers through my hair. "Cotton picking season is finished so the migrant labors are no longer needed. That's why la migra took them away. It's also the reason why I must continue working at the refinery, no matter what trouble comes."

Papá smelled of oil and sweat, but I knew that it was the smell of love. I glanced out my window at the lighted, question mark tower at the refinery. Where are Roberto and María now? I wondered.

Chapter IX
WHAT'S THIS GAME
THAT MAKES PEOPLE LOCO?

September brought cooler weather to Oak Grove. The elms and willows along the river had streaks of yellow or brown. Some nights I lay awake, listening to dry corn leaves rustling in Mamá's garden, and wondered what this month would bring. Will the United States go to war? Will all the refinery workers except Papá go on strike?

But the people of our community shoved those questions aside and talked about nothing except football. Oak Grove had the best team in its league except, maybe, Laguna. Everyone was asking, "Can we win the championship this year?"

"What's this game that makes people loco?" Papá asked at breakfast one Saturday morning. "I know they call it football, but it's different from the way it's played in Mexico and most other countries."

"In football Americano," I explained between bites, "they don't use a round ball but one that looks like this." Getting up from the table, I took an egg from the ice box and held it up between two fingers.

"Then they should call it egg ball," Papá said.

Everyone laughed. "The shape of the ball isn't the only difference between soccer and football Americano," said Violeta.

She, Rosita, and I tried to explain the game while moving knives, forks, glasses and salt and pepper shakers around the table to represent football players. Papá looked even more confused. "I still don't get it," he said, pulling at his mustache. "You have eleven people on one team. They run with the ball instead of passing it from player to player with their feet. And the other team tries to kill whoever is carrying the ball. No wonder he throws it to someone else."

Even though Papá didn't understand football, he let us older kids go to the game on Friday because it was free to students. The twins walked to the stadium with their friends. Owl and I arrived there on our bicycles just as the overhead lights came on.

We sat down in the stands as our team trotted

onto the field in red and white uniforms. The cheerleaders, dressed in those same colors, jumped up and down in front of our bleachers yelling, "Yeah, Roughnecks! Go, Roughnecks! Go! Go! Go!"

Our team was named Roughnecks because the men who did the tough, dangerous job of drilling for oil were called that. A lot of Oak Grove people worked in the oil fields.

The other team came from Rancho Grande. They were the "Vaqueros," a Spanish word meaning "Cowboys."

Wearing white jerseys and black pants, they did their jumping-jacks at the far end of the field. Not many people sat in the visitor stands, so I could barely hear them chanting for a Vaqueros victory.

Two captains from each team met with the referee who tossed a coin. The Roughnecks received the ball and ran the kickoff back for a touchdown. They kicked the ball through the goal post for the extra point and led 7 to 0 in the first two or three minutes of the game. At halftime, when the bands marched onto the field, Oak Grove had 35 and Rancho 0.

During the second half, our "B" team continued to make points against the Vaqueros.

Owl and I started watching the game taking place beneath the bleachers. Some sixth-grade boys there were tossing a jacket tied into a ball with strings. "Wanta play?"I asked.

"Anything's better than watching this slaughter," Owl said, leading the way down from the stands.

"We get Richard!" both teams yelled until someone flipped a coin.

"Oh shucks," said the captain who lost the toss. "Come on, Jose," he said reluctantly as though I had the measles or something.

I played okay, though, and wasn't chosen last anymore. On Fridays when the Roughnecks played at home, we younger kids had our own little game of football under the bleachers.

There wasn't much light, so we had to be careful not to bump our heads on the rafters. We sometimes tripped over bottles and other trash covering the ground. The only injury, though, came when someone in the stands dropped a bottle of Coca Cola on me.

Lying there on my back, I couldn't see anything but stars. As my head cleared, I looked up at the rows of feet. Then I spotted T-Rex's round face, grinning down at me from between the benches.

Owl shook the half-full bottle of cola and squirted it up at him. Only T-Rex moved and the wet, sticky stuff landed on the bare legs of several women sitting there. They screamed and called us "filthy brats." A little while later, Sheriff Madfellow showed up and chased us from under the stands.

At midnight when Papá came in to kiss me good night, he examined the knot on my head. "Qué pasó, Jose?"

I didn't mention the Coke bottle because that'd make Papá really mad, and maybe he wouldn't let me go to any more football games. "I got hurt playing under the bleachers."

"They were made to sit on, Mijo."

Oak Grove won all their games in September and well into October. We'd win the Class A championship if we could beat Laguna High School. They hadn't lost in football for as long as anyone could remember. "The Sharks will swallow the Roughnecks," wrote the sports editor in the Corpus Christi Caller.

They arrived at Oak Grove that Friday before Halloween.

Right after school, Owl and I rode our bikes downtown and saw them. The Laguna kids piled off three busses and lined up on Main Street.

The first two students carried a banner which said, "SEVENTY-TWO STRAIGHT VICTORIES. OAK GROVE MAKES SEVENTY-THREE."

Behind them a row of cheerleaders twisted and tossed their shiny batons, their gold and white dresses sparkling in the late-afternoon sun. The band, too, marched in uniforms of those colors, playing the Shark's fight song. Then came the football team of forty or fifty boys, all laughing and cracking jokes.

"They're big," I said.

"Giants!" Owl added as we watched them parade down the street and into the high school stadium.

Owl and I climbed into the bleachers early that evening so we could get a good seat in the middle of the top row. Soon everyone in town was there, screaming and whistling as the Roughnecks trotted out of the clubhouse in a long red-and-white line. The other stands were filled with Shark fans, cheering as their team took the field for their warmups. This game would determine the Class A championship.

By halftime, neither team had scored. Owl bought us a popcorn and a soda while we watched the bands perform. They were really loud, especially the drums which called the warring teams back onto the field.

The third quarter crept by, and the score still stood at 0 to 0.

With five minutes left to play, the Roughnecks completed a long pass which put them inside the Sharks' ten yard line with a first down and goal to go. After three failed runs, our team was still there.

What to do now? Anyone else would have kicked a field goal, but the Roughnecks hadn't completed a single one this season.

We all held our breath as the quarterback took the ball from the center and backed up a couple of yards. Then, in a surprise move, the center shot up the middle of the field and received the pass. He squirmed past the Sharks who hit him from all sides. Staggering across the goal line, he was brought down by another Shark, then their whole team piled on him.

The Oak Grove fans screamed and jumped up and down so much I thought the stands would fall.

Our team bounced around on the field, hugging each other, all except one. Number 24, Salvador García, lay in the end zone where he had been brought down after making a touchdown for the Roughnecks. I knew him because his father, like mine, worked at the refinery.

Everyone in the bleachers got quiet as Salvador's team mates crowded around him. The coach ran out and made them back up. The announcer called for a doctor.

"I want to get closer," I said, and started down the stands with Owl right behind me.

When we got to the side lines, Dr. Goldstein was kneeling beside Salvador who kept groaning and saying, "My leg! My leg!"

The physician took a syringe from his black bag and gave Sal a shot. "You'll feel better now," he said, then beckoned for the ambulance.

The driver, standing next to it, didn't move. The coach ran over to him, and the two began arguing and shaking their fists at each other. "I can't take him in the ambulance," shouted the man in white. "What if someone else gets hurt?"

Finally, two men slid Salvador onto a stretcher then lifted him into the back of the pickup. As it drove away, everyone stood up and chanted "Sal-va-dor! Sal-va-dor!"

The game ended three minutes later with Oak Grove winning 7 to 0. Only then did the ambulance move.

Even though Oak Grove won the Class A championship, I felt sad. At midnight when Papá came into my room I was standing at the window, staring at the question mark in the sky. "What are you thinking about, Mijo?" he asked.

"Salvador's leg got broken, but the ambulance driver wouldn't take him to the hospital."

Papá pulled at his mustache. "What's this game that makes people loco?" he said, leaving the room.

Chapter X
WHAT'S A TRICKER TREE?

At school we moved from one holiday to the next, much like climbing a ladder. First came Halloween. In a way it wasn't even a holiday. We still had to go to school. But many kids thought that, except for Christmas, Halloween was the best day of the year. For me, it just brought another problem.

The trouble started that Friday morning. Since it was Papá's day off work, the family had breakfast together. Everyone was already mad at me because I sat down late, then had get up to comb my hair. But I asked anyway. "Papá, I am twelve years old, and I've never gone trick-or-treating. Por favor, please, may I go tonight?"

He shook his fork at me, scattering eggs all over the table. "No! Every year you ask the same question, and every year I tell you the same answer. You can go from house to house begging for candy when you are old enough to live under your own roof."

"You won't need a costume then," said Violeta, "because you'll be grey-headed and have a long beard."

Across the table, the twins grinned at me like identical apes. "Are you going to have fun at the dance tonight?" I asked them.

"Papá?" they both pleaded.

"No! No! No!" he said, twitching his mustache. "It is not permitted for you to go out before your quinceañera."

"But our birthday comes in only one month," argued Violeta.

Before Papá could answer, a loud knock rattled the door.

"Ricardo," said Mamá, shaking her head. "Why does he always come while we're having breakfast?"

"Because he likes your tortillas," I said, starting to get up.

But Marikita darted to the door and swung it open. "Buenos días, Ricardo," she greeted Owl, leading him by the hand into the kitchen where we were eating. "You make a tricker tree tonight?"

Everyone laughed. "Marikita, it's not something you make," I said. "Trick or treat is something you do."

"No," she said, sitting back down and crossing her arms. "It's like a Christmas tree, only for Halloween."

By now we'd all greeted Owl. Mamá pulled up a chair for him. "Thanks," he mumbled, working on the platter of tortillas like he was getting paid for making them disappear.

As I followed Owl out the front door, Mamá said, "Te portas bien, Mijo."

"Sí, Mamá."

"I'll have to be good," I told Owl as I pushed my bike from the garage. "Papá says if I get in trouble again, he'll sell my bicycle."

School was never fun for me on Halloween. When I was little, we made pictures of ghosts and witches to decorate our classroom. Since I couldn't draw worth beans, the other kids always made fun of my work.

This Halloween in art class we carved scary faces on pumpkins. Owl and I were partners until he started playing catapult with his ruler. "Boom!" he shouted, as a big glob of seeds shot into the air and plopped down on Ruth Ann's head. She screamed as if she'd sat on a tack, and so did the teacher. Even though I didn't do anything, Mrs. Miller made me help Owl clean up the mess and apologize to Ruth Ann.

I was still angry at him after school, but he acted as though he hadn't gotten me into trouble. "Race you to the top of the hill," he said as we climbed on our bicycles.

The hill three miles south of town was the highest one in all of Oak County. As I puffed up it, I found Owl sitting under a mesquite in the cemetery. "What kept you?" he asked as I dropped down beside him.

"You have a new bike," I reminded him.

The stone monuments went out from the highway in long rows. Some of them stood as tall as the ticket booth at the county fair. But mostly just wooden crosses, scattered along the back fence, marked the Mexican section.

Owl chewed on a piece of grass. "Will you come here tomorrow to put candy on the graves?" he asked.

He was talking about the Day of the Dead which many Mexicans celebrate. "No, we don't have any relatives buried here."

"But do you think your dead really eat the candy people put on their graves?"

For a long time I just sat there looking at the river looping its way across the valley like a brown snake. Some of the trees along its bank still held onto their leaves, but many looked like skeletons. The fields, too, had turned brown with only a few green patches of oats scattered among them. And to the north, the houses of Oak Grove appeared as toys. Behind them stood the oil tanks at the refinery, glistening in the sun, and the black tower that looked like a question mark.

"Cat got your tongue?" Owl asked.

"I guess our dead can eat the candy we put on their graves on El Día de Los Muertos, if your dead can smell the flowers you leave for them on Memorial Day."

"Tricky, Tricky!" he said, getting up and brushing the dirt from his bottom. "You'd make a good lawyer. Come on. I want to see if Mom is finished with my scary crow costume."

I thought Owl meant scarecrow, a straw man like the one standing in our garden to chase away the birds. But that night when he walked to our house wearing the costume, I saw that it really was a scary crow. The long sleeves were shaped like wings, and the mask had a yellow beak. "It's nice," I said. "Maybe I should call you Crow instead of Owl."

"I'm Crow only this one night," he said, laughing.

After he left, I lay on my bed feeling sorry for myself because I couldn't go trick-or-treating. Then Marikita sneaked into my room. "Boo!" she said, trying to scare me. "Jose, por favor, make me a tricker-tree."

At the kitchen table I helped her color some lunch sacks with an orange crayola. Then we drew faces on the bags, blew air into them, and hung our paper jack-o-lanterns on the chinaberry tree in the back yard. "Gracias," Marikita said, with a smile on her face as big as the full moon peeking over the horizon.

Before following my little sister back into the house, I looked toward the refinery at the question mark in the sky. Swish swish, swish swish, went the steam pumps. What next? What next? they seemed to say.

Chapter XI
WHAT'S A FRIEND?

One morning, Miss Rose paced back and forth in front of the classroom with a stick of chalk in her hand. "I don't want you to tell me who your friends are," she said. "I already know that by whom you're with every day." She smiled at Owl and I sitting together near the back. He rolled his eyes which made me giggle.

"This is your essay topic for today." Our literature teacher wrote, "What is a friend?" on the chalkboard behind her. "What are some ideas you associate with friendship?"

Kids began calling out words, and Miss Rose wrote them on the chalkboard: loyal, nice, companion, kind. After the list covered half of the board, our teacher said, "Tonight you'll write a paper titled, 'What is a Friend?' And tomorrow I'll call on you to read your magnificent papers aloud."

There were groans followed by a few laughs.

But everyone roared when Ralph drawled, "I don't know how to write an essay."

Frank thought he did. Grinning, he quickly copied the dictionary definition of friend and slapped his paper down on Miss Rose's big, wooden desk. After glancing at it, she handed it back. "I want at least one page," she said, "and it has to be your work, not Mr. Webster's."

When Norman rang the dismissal bell that afternoon, we darted out of math class. The sun hung well above the horizon. "There's still time to get into trouble," Owl said, jumping on his bike. So instead of going straight home, we rode to the forks of the rivers.

That was another one of our favorite places. Two miles south of town, the Río Frío joined the Brown River which flowed on, deep and muddy, to the Gulf of Mexico. Along its banks grew ash, elms, and other trees, all tangled with grape vines. Owl and I swung on one of the loose vines, yelling like Tarzan.

When we got tired of that, we just sat on the bank, watching the river. Some alligator gars splashed in the brown waters. Those fish had long snouts and rows of sharp teeth.

A couple of snapping turtles sat on a log beside the stream. "They say that if one bites you, it won't turn loose until it thunders," I said.

"Hear it?" Owl asked, his head cocked.

I just heard a chattering noise. "It's up there," I said, pointing to a little gray animal jumping from limb to limb high in a Live Oak.

"Not the squirrel. Thunder."

Dark clouds piled up overhead as the norther moved in with its icy wind blowing long strands of moss from the oaks. As we rode out of the woods, big, cold drops of rain splashed down on us. Just before we reached the highway, we came to an abandoned cabin. Jumping off our bikes, we raced inside. The shack was empty, or so we thought.

The walls were made of railroad ties and covered with a tin roof. The rain beat against it with such a roar we could scarcely hear ourselves talk. "Smells musty in here," shouted Owl.

He was about to pick up a railroad spike from one of the shelves lining the back wall when I saw the rattler coiled up beside it. "Snake!" I yelled, almost jerking Owl's arm out of its socket as I pulled him back.

For a few seconds we just stood there as though hypnotized. Its tail was a blur of motion, the flat head with the little beady eyes raised above the coils, its tongue darting in and out.

Owl and I both charged through the open door at the same time. Bumping into each other, we fell flat on our faces outside.

Sitting in the mud, we laughed until tears mixed with the rain on our cheeks. Finally the shower passed. But as we rode away, we heard the angry snake still buzzing inside the shelter.

At home the sewing machine clattered a different tune. Quinceañera, quinceañera, it seemed to say as Mamá slid a silky white dress under speeding needle and thread. Her foot moved the pedal up and down so fast I could hardly see it. "Where have you been?" she asked without looking up.

"With Ricardo," I said, hurrying into my room before she noticed my wet, muddy clothes.

After I showered and changed, I found Marikita playing paper dolls at the kitchen table. "Hola, Jose," she said, smiling. "Quieres jugar conmigo?"

"No, I don't play dolls. Besides, I'm hungry."

Like a little mother, Marikita jumped up and brought my sandwich from the ice box and even poured me a glass of milk. As I sat there eating, I watched her playing. Holding up one doll, then another, she spoke for them in Spanish. Her dimpled cheeks and sparkling eyes reminded me of the the cheerful sunflowers on the table cloth which seemed to dance as the kerosene lamp flickered.

I turned the handle on its side to raise the wick. The smell of kerosene oil grew stronger but so did the light. Now I could see well enough to do my homework.

The next morning, Miss Rose called on me first to read my essay. I walked to the front of the class and looked at Owl, sitting in the back. He rolled his eyes.

"A friend is someone you care about and who cares about you. He's someone you do fun things with such as playing, swimming, and riding bicycles. A friend is someone you can talk to and tell secrets. He won't tease you even when you do dumb things, like singing, 'Jose, can you see'. " The whole class laughed. "A friend is someone you can always count on to be there when you need him."

Most of the kids clapped politely as I took my seat. But they roared with laughter when Owl stood by his desk and read, "A friend is someone who keeps you from getting bit by a rattlesnake."

"Would you like to explain that?" asked Miss Rose.

Owl told about yesterday's adventure even

though he had written only one sentence on his paper. I guess Miss Rose wasn't impressed because he got an "F" on the assignment.

That night I looked out my bedroom window at the question-mark tower. Things were not going well at the refinery. Owl's father and a group of men had walked away from their jobs while my father and a few others continued to work. Could the strike keep Owl and me from being friends?

Chapter XII
WHAT'S THAT SMELL?

The real trouble started that Sunday, November 1, 1941.

I awoke to rain splashing against my window. Looking out, I couldn't see the question mark. Water stood in the plowed rows of Mamá's garden, I heard frogs croaking. More rain! More rain! they seemed to say.

After mass, I worked on my "theme" assignment for Miss Rose. In the afternoon, I became bored with studying and went to work with Papá.

We walked to the refinery, like he always did, no matter what the weather. "Mamá might need the car," Papá said.

Darkness came early, and our rain slickers reflected the street lights. In the refinery parking lot we were stopped by some men waving signs about unfair wages. I recognized only Owl's father, a large, blond-headed man, carrying an umbrella and yelling something about getting more people to strike. Grabbing Papá by the arm, he said, "Are you with us, Jose?"

Papá shook his head. "Dutch, I don't get paid for carrying a sign. My job is firing boilers."

The big, rusty things hissed in the rain. At first I was afraid to go near them. What if one of them explodes? I thought. But, finally, I joined Papá in the little tin shed which stood facing the boilers. It was mostly empty except for some rusty tools hanging along one wall and a couple of straw chairs. They looked old and ragged as if they'd been dragged from the city dump.

I sat in one and Papá in the other. Every few minutes he glanced through the open doorway at the gauges on the boilers. "The pressure is too low," Papá explained, "because the rain cools the boilers."

S-w-i-s-h, s-w-i-s-h went the two big pumps nearest us, their arms moving back and forth in slow motion. "There isn't enough steam for both of them," Papá said, going out the door. When he closed the valve of the first pump, the second picked up speed. Swish, swish, swish, swish.

Everything at the refinery smelled, tasted, and felt oily. Crude oil dripped from the pipes running everywhere and mixed with dirt on the ground. That gooey mess stuck to my shoes and jumped on my pants. I sat in the boiler shed rubbing a big glob from the cuff of my new jeans onto the chair leg. "Jose, tu mamá va a matarte," said Papá, twisting his mustache.

"She doesn't kill you when you get dirty."

Before he could answer, a big tanker truck snorted up the unloading ramp across the street from the boilers. Papá attached a big hose to the bottom of its tank and started a pump which sucked out the oil.

By then, the driver had gone home, so my father had to move the truck. I sat beside him in the cab, staring at the lighted instruments, while he drove the big rig into the parking lot across the road east of the refinery. Shhhhh, sounded the air brakes, like Mrs. Dozier trying to get the class quiet.

We didn't see Dutch or any of the other strikers. "Where have they gone?" I asked Papá.

"Quién sabe – who knows?" he said. "Maybe they got tired of standing in the rain.

Back in the hut, I curled up in my chair. The heat and roar of the boilers made me doze until I felt Papá's hand on my shoulder. "Jose, I'm going to the river."

"I'll come, too," I said, yawning.

We followed the winding path through the dark woods with only Papá's flashlight to show us the way. Finally we came to the river bank and another tin shed not much bigger than a dog house.

"The electric pump is inside," said Papá. He pulled the lever on a pole, and the machine began humming. "It pumps water to the storage tanks at the refinery. From there it goes into the boilers to make steam. They use a lot of water."

I listened to it splashing over the dam. The sky had cleared, and I saw stars reflected in the dark river.

Then I heard a loud crack that sounded like a shot, but I guess it was just a stick breaking. When Papá shined his light around, I noticed some of the bushes moving. Trembling, I began to back toward the river. It's probably a mountain lion! I thought, my heart pounding in my throat.

Suddenly white balls rained down on us. When they exploded against our clothing and on the ground around us, they stank like the burning-sulfur experiment we did last year in science. The stench of the rotten eggs caused me to gag.

Someone in the woods laughed. I recognized

the voice of Owl's father. "Better join us, Jose," he said, "or something worse than this might happen to you."

"Nunca! Nunca! Nunca!" yelled Papá. "Never will I strike the hand that feeds me."

Stinking like rotten eggs, we hurried back to the refinery to clean up. There were two bathrooms, one for white men and the other for Mexicans. In ours, someone had written on the mirror with soap, "Remember the Alamo!"

"What does it mean?" I asked Papá.

"It means someone doesn't like Mexicans," he said.

Papá and I showered there with our clothes on, trying to get them clean. But when we got home, they still stank so we threw them into the garbage can. Then we showered again until we ran out of hot water.

I didn't get much sleep after that. The "Jose, can you see?" dream kept spinning through my mind until daylight finally came.

When it was time for school, Owl didn't come for me and wasn't in the chair swing by his house where he sometimes waited. I wondered why he'd gone without me. As I parked my bike in the long wooden rack next to his, he strolled over toward me with some other boys.

"There he is," said T-Rex, nudging him. "Do it."

Looking at me, Owl sniffed the air like a hound dog. "What's that smell?" he asked.

His new friends all laughed as if he'd told the world's funniest joke.

I quickly walked away so they wouldn't see my tears.

Owl and I didn't sit together in any of our classes. Riding home alone that afternoon, I looked at the question mark tower and wondered, Will Owl ever be my friend again?

Chapter XIII
WHOSE FAULT WAS IT?

I didn't know whose fault it was, but it must have been mine. Everyone said it was.

The trouble began Tuesday morning right after I got to school. Owl stood with some other boys just outside Mrs. Dozier's classroom. As I walked up, he sniffed at me again and asked, "What's that smell?" All the kids waiting there laughed, even some of the girls.

School started with a Mexican head check. First, a messenger from the office came for Juanita. A little while later, Juanita returned to homeroom, blushing like she had a sun burn. She handed the note to me.

When I walked through the nurse's door, I found her office crowded with Mexican children from the elementary school up the street. Some of the little kids cried because they thought they were getting a shot. But having their heads checked for lice wasn't much better.

One of the ladies poked around in my hair with a pencil, then said, "You're clean today, Jose." When I returned to homeroom, the kids snickered. I felt like I'd just been slapped.

Things didn't go well for me in language arts either. Miss Rose assigned us to write a poem about feelings. I'd barely started mine when Johnny snatched it from my desk and read outloud. "I feel so alone since my friend is gone. Days of gladness have turned to sadness."

Everyone laughed, and my face burned with embarrassment again.

At lunch recess, I went back to the language arts room to work on our theme assignment, which was due before Christmas vacation. Miss Rose helped me with my English until Joey knocked on the door.

"Can Jose come out?" he asked. "We need him on our soccer team."

I didn't want to go, but my teacher smiled and said, "Sure. All work and no play makes Jose a dull boy."

The boys on the field formed two lines as the captains chose their teams. "We have Jose!" called Butch.

Owl stood with the other team, along with T-Rex and some of his new friends. Two boys from each side threw down their jackets to make the goal boxes. Except for the end zones, we had no boundaries.

In the center of the field the captains kicked at the ball, but mostly just clobbered each other's shins. I jabbed it with my right foot, faked around Owl, and kicked it past T-Rex through the goal box. My team cheered because we led one to zero. But a few minutes later Owl scored. It was still a tie game when someone kicked the ball into the street.

"I'll get it!" I shouted, darting through the gate.

"No, it's our ball," Owl said, following me into the street where we struggled over it. The yard duty teacher didn't see us until a car honked. Mr. Bradshaw rushed over and grabbed each of us by the arm and led us to the office.

About that time, Norman stepped out of Mrs. Dozier's room, clanging her bell. Owl and I missed both social studies and math, waiting all afternoon in the principal's office. I read all of the degrees and plaques hanging on the wall, but my mind kept returning to the soccer ball in the street.

"I called for it," I said. "Why didn't you let me bring it in?"

Owl glared at me. "Just shut up, Jose. It was our ball."

Finally, Mr. Tuffit arrived about ten minutes before school was dismissed. Frowning, he read the note from Mr. Bradshaw. "Fighting over a soccer ball in the street? Well, boys, what do you have to say about that?"

Both Owl and I shrugged.

"All right. You're not to play soccer anymore this month. And you'd better stay out of trouble."

Mrs. Dozier's bell rang. "I wonder what we missed in math," I said as Owl and I left the principal's office.

"Who cares?" he said.

I ran to the classroom and got our assignment while Owl waited at the bike rack with some other boys. When I handed him his math book, he just threw it down. I didn't see T-Rex drop to his knees behind me. But when Owl shoved me backwards, I fell over him. Then I lost my temper.

I kicked the dinosaur in his side and punched Owl's nose. It bled so much that we both got smeared with blood as we wrestled on the ground. The kids made a huddle around us, shouting, "Fight! Fight! Fight!"

"Break it up!" screamed a couple of the women teachers. "Stop that fighting, Jose!" But Owl and I continued hitting each other until Mr. Tuffit dragged us back into his office.

He called Mr. Krause who came for his son. When Owl's father saw me standing there all covered with blood, he smiled. "Good job, Richard!"

Since I didn't have a telephone, the principal drove me home in his Buick. "Don't get blood on the seats," he said.

Papá was getting ready to leave for work when Mr. Tuffit met him on the front porch and told him about the fight. "I will not tolerate that conduct in my school," he said. "Jose is suspended until next Monday."

After the principal drove away, I thought Papá would ask if I was hurt. Instead, he shouted, "Why did you fight, Jose?"

I was shaking all over and crying so hard I couldn't answer.

For a long time, Papá just stood there, pulling on his mustache. Then he stomped off toward the refinery. He wouldn't even get into the car with us as Mamá drove me back to school for my bicycle. Someone had cut the tires, so I had to push it home.

I guess Papá was still angry with me when he came home at midnight because he didn't come into my room. I looked out my window at the question mark outlined with lights against the dark sky. Your fault, your fault, hissed the steam pumps, and I cried some more.

Chapter XIV
WHERE DO I BELONG?

Mr. Tuffit told my father that I didn't belong at school, not until I learned to stop fighting. But I didn't seem to belong at home either.

Everyone else had something to do. When Violeta and Rosita weren't at school, they stayed in their room, studying. Papá worked two shifts at the refinery now that so many were out on strike. He came home at midnight, slept a few hours, then returned to work every morning at 8:00.

Mamá stayed busy making dresses for the twins and other girls who would be in the quinceañera. When I watched her too long, she became nervous. "Jose, por favor, find something to do."

"What, Mamá?"

"Tú puedes jugar conmigo," said Marikita, cradling a doll in her arms.

I shook my head. "I don't play dolls."

In the afternoon I pulled a chair up close to our big, wooden radio and listened to my favorite program, "Jack Armstrong, the All American Boy." He was a hero who, unlike me, never did anything wrong. I knew that I wasn't an "all-American boy," but I wasn't all-Mexican either.

I found that out every time I went to Mexico. My favorite uncle had a farm near Monterey, but most of my relatives were poor and lived in Nuevo Laredo. I hated it there where cardboard shacks lined the dirt streets.

My cousins and I played soccer and spoke the same language. But many other of our customs were different. They didn't know about Halloween, Thanksgiving, and the Fourth of July. And in school they recited everything out loud. The adobe building had only one room except for the two outhouses in the back.

At my school, many of the teachers seemed to think that all Mexicans were alike. I didn't know why they believed that. We didn't all dress alike or eat the same foods. Papá liked his meat spicy with lots of chiles. Mamá couldn't stand peppers. "They give me indigestion," she said.

Feeling really bored one cold day, I walked to Mexican town. It was part of Oak Grove, yet different. Located next to the refinery, everything smelled of oil. The unpaved streets were lined with shacks only a little better than those I'd seen in Nuevo Laredo. Clothes hung drying on the lines, getting dirty again from blowing dust. Young children in ragged clothes played barefooted in their yards. Lean dogs ran around everywhere, barking. I certainly don't belong here, I thought.

On the edge of that community I met an old man wearing a black coat and hat. "Está frío," he said, which, in proper Spanish, meant that something, such as an ice cube, was cold.

"Sí, hace frío," I answered him, saying that the weather was cold.

How long will it be before I forget how to speak Spanish? I wondered.

Back home, I warmed by the iron stove in the kitchen until Mamá said, "We need more wood, Jose."

Outside, the blue smoke and smell of burning mesquite drifted down from the chimney. I found Papá's big ax in the tool shed and saw that it was dull. I sat down on the iron stool which was cold as ice. Está frío, I thought, peddling furiously to keep the grinding wheel spinning. Sparks flew from the ax head as I sharpened one side, then the other until the edge felt like Papá's razor.

The logs in the wood pile had to be cut smaller to fit inside our stove. I chopped until my hands were sore and red. Then I carried several armloads of sticks into the kitchen and dropped them into the wood box. I also brought in a bucket of chips which Mamá used to kindle the fire every morning.

Later that afternoon, I stood on the porch watching Owl ride his bicycle home from school. We both waved. He started to walk over, but his father shouted, "Richard, get back here!"

Late that night I heard a tap on my window. When I stepped outside, there wasn't anyone there. But on the porch I found a pile of books and notes from my teachers, giving their assignments. I worked on them until almost midnight. Then, early the next morning while it was still dark, I left my homework on the chair swing under the mesquite by Owl's house. We made that exchange in silence for the rest of the week.

Since I did most of my school work at night, I would have been bored during the day except for my little sister. One morning I awoke with her standing at my bedside, grinning. "Jose, you teach me to read?" she asked.

I made word cards of paper, like my first grade teacher used to do, and taped them to things all over the house: table, chair, radio, wall, bed. Marikita used them in sentences, which I wrote on a tablet for her to read. *This is a bed. That is a radio.*

Marikita learned to recognize words really fast, but it was harder teaching her to speak English correctly.

"Marikita is a bad girl," I joked.

"No, she not."

"No, she isn't," I corrected. "Marikita is a good girl."

"Yes, she is."

Marikita beamed like a sun flower every time she answered correctly. I praised and hugged her for trying so hard. Without even knowing it, my little sister cheered me up more than anything else during those three days I was suspended from school.

Papá must have forgiven me for fighting because, on Saturday, he took me to San Antonio with him. All that morning our Model A Ford clattered along at 30 M.P.H. Finally, the green farms gave way to houses and then to buildings so tall they seemed to touch the sky.

Surrounded by these sky scrapers stood an old Spanish mission. "The Alamo," a sign said.

"Papá, can we stop and see it?"

"Por qué, Mijo?"

"Because of that writing on the bathroom mirror at the refinery, Remember the Alamo."

We parked on the next block and walked back to the famous church. Inside the stone chapel everyone spoke in a whisper, and the men took off their hats.

The Alamo had a museum, too, with lots of old muskets and sabers used in the Texas War of Independence. Standing under a large Texas flag, a guide told us about the battle fought here in 1836. With thin gray hair and a wrinkled face, she looked old enough to have seen it.

"The chapel is the only remaining building of the mission complex," she said. "For thirteen days, two hundred Texas volunteers fought off General Santa Anna's army of several thousand men. But just before sunrise on March 6, the Mexican soldiers finally scaled the walls and killed all of the Alamo's defenders."

I raised my hand. "Were any of the defenders Mexicans?"

She nodded. "Several of them died here, fighting for Texas. How old are you, Son?"

"Twelve, Ma'am."

"When Santa Anna's troops stormed into the chapel, they found Enrique Esparza. Like you, he was twelve and small for his age. Maybe that was why the soldiers spared him after killing his father and the other Texas volunteers."

I looked at the stone walls, cracked with age, and thought about how sad Enrique must have felt about the death of his father.

Then I spotted Papá in the doorway, beckoning to me. "We came to the big city to make the arrangements for the twins' quinceañera," he reminded me as we walked away from the Alamo. "Their birthday is only a week away."

In one of the stores Papá rented a tuxedo for him and me. "Qué guapo!" he said, when I tried on the black suit in front of the mirror. I thought he looked handsome in his, too.

We went into another building where Papá paid for a band to play music at the party. Papá spent a lot of money that day. "Now you won't have enough to buy those golf clubs," I joked on the way home.

"I still have a little," he said, pulling into a drive-in restaurant. A young lady wearing shorts came out on roller skates to take our order.

"Two hamburgers with fries and milkshakes chocolate," he said

About midnight we drove down our dark lane, past Owl's house and into our garage. It felt good to be home. This is where I belonged. But when I looked at the question mark outlined with lights, I wondered what school would be like on Monday. Will I belong there, too?

When I went to sleep, I had that "Jose, can you see?" nightmare again.

Chapter XV
WHO'LL COME TO THE PARTY?

After early mass, Sunday, my family gathered at the breakfast table in the kitchen. As usual, our conversation turned to the twins' fifteenth birthday celebration coming up in just six days. Papá told about the wonderful band he'd hired to perform at the party. Mamá said that the dresses were almost finished. Marikita wanted to know about the dolls her sisters would give to her at the quinceañera. "Are they beautiful?" she asked.

The twins seemed nervous as they pushed their huevos and chorizos – eggs and sausages– around their plates with a tortilla. "Are you playing breakfast hockey?" asked Papá, frowning.

Then Violeta dropped their secret like a bomb. "We don't want a quinceañera," she said, looking at her twin for support.

"No, we don't want it," said Rosita, shaking her head.

"Qué? Qué?" shouted Papá, tugging at his mustache.

Then both girls ran to their room, sobbing. Mamá followed them, calling, "Don't worry about it. You're just nervous."

The señoritas had almost stopped crying when Papá charged into their room, yelling loud enough for the whole world to hear, "You will have this quinceañera!" There was a lot more shouting and arguing.

"I can't believe this is happening," I told Marikita who was still sitting at the table with me. She looked like she was about to cry, also.

Except for her wedding, the quinceañera was the most important celebration in a Mexican girl's life. After that, she could wear lipstick and go on dates. The twins had been talking about their special day and planning it for as long as I could remember. Why would they want to give it up now?

Papá had spent hundreds of dollars arranging for the fiesta. Mamá worked on the dresses forever. "We already sent out the invitations," I heard her say.

One of the twins yelled, "Who will come to our party?"

So that was the problem. The twins, too, had

lost friends because Papá didn't support the strike at the refinery. No wonder they'd fled from the table crying.

While waiting for another outburst from the bedroom, I began counting the sun flowers on the tablecloth with my little sister.

"One."

"One," she repeated.

"Two."

"Two," she said with big tears sliding down her dimpled cheeks. "I'm never going to have a quinceañera."

"Me neither." Biting a hole in the middle of my tortilla, I peeked at Marikita through it.

She grinned back at me. "Boys don't have quinceañeras," she said.

After a few minutes, the arguing in the girls' room ended, and the rest of the family marched back into the kitchen to finish breakfast. "Pásame los huevos, por favor," Papá said.

I passed him the eggs. "Well, are we having the fiesta or not?"

Mamá smiled. "Sí, even if we have to bring the guests from another country."

Neither we nor our relatives in Mexico had telephones, and there wasn't enough time to write them before the quinceañera. For that reason, Mamá and Marikita boarded the train early Monday morning for Nuevo Laredo. "We'll be back late Wednesday," said Mamá, kissing me on the cheek.

I stood by the tracks waving until I could see only a thin trail of white smoke on the horizon. Then I hurried to school, wondering if I smelled like coal dust.

On his way to work Wednesday evening, Papá left the twins and me at the depot, sitting in our old Ford. Finally, we heard a train whistling in the distance and climbed outside to watch. With its large bell clanging on top, the steam engine chugged into the station, pulling four passenger cars. Mamá got off the last one, struggling with a heavy suitcase in one hand and a sleeping Marikita in the other. Racing to her, I picked up my little sister while the twins took turns carrying the luggage. "It's been arranged," Mamá told them. "You'll have your escorts."

I had never seen my big sisters so happy. On the way home they sat in the back seat, chattering like identical monkeys.

At school that week Owl and I avoided each other. Sometimes we met in the corridor or lunch area, but we didn't smile or speak. Papá had told me, "Stay away from Ricardo!" I guess his father said the same thing about me, or maybe he didn't need to. Anyway, our friendship was dead.

At home, I gave up my bed to an uncle and aunt, then slept on the floor with my cousins and other relatives from Mexico. I didn't sleep much, though, with all that snoring going on. It shook the whole house so that even the windows vibrated. So many people lay on blankets that I couldn't get up to go to the bathroom without stepping on someone.

In the daytime, the women stayed busy making everything from dresses to tamales. "Quinceañera, quinceañera," was all they talked about. I got so sick of hearing that word I stayed out of the house all I could. Sometimes I watched the men sitting around a table on the front porch playing dominoes. But mostly I played soccer with my cousins in the empty field behind our house.

Once I saw Owl staring at us from his chair swing. I wanted to ask him to join us, then thought of Papá. I was sure Owl's father wouldn't let him come over anyway, so there wasn't any point in inviting him. I waved at him, though, and he returned the greeting.

By the end of the week, a lot of Violeta and

Rosita's friends had answered the invitations saying that they were coming to the party. Filled with happiness, the twins bounced around the house, chattering with everyone about the quinceañera. But Mamá looked worried. "Maybe there won't be enough food," she told Papá.

Frantically, Mamá and my aunts made more tamales. Pots of frijoles – beans – cooked on the wood stove while others sat on the kitchen table, soaking. Outside, my uncles barbecued beef over a pit of coals. The aroma drifted into the house and made my mouth water.

Friday night, most of the family sat in the living room talking, too excited about the quinceañera to sleep. I couldn't sleep either, but for a different reason. Soon, my cousins would return to Mexico, and I'd be alone again. I wondered if Owl and I would ever be friends again.

Chapter XVI
WHO'S THE LITTLE ANGEL?

I dreamed that we were at war. Bombs exploded all around me, lighting up the whole countryside. I awoke trembling and covered with sweat.

In the next room Marikita cried out, and Mamá rushed to her bedside. "It's just thunder, Mija. Go back to sleep."

For a long time I lay awake, listening to the rain pounding against our tin roof. We weren't at war, but I kept thinking about that nightmare. It was like a warning that something bad would happen.

But Saturday morning that gloomy feeling had passed with the storm. Mamá called the whole family outside to see a beautiful rainbow which arched across the sky to the north. "God sent it to decorate your special day," she told the twins.

The quinceañera started at church that afternoon with a service of thanksgiving, "Mass Acción de Gracias." The rows were filled with people dressed in their finest. The smell of ladies' perfume mixed with that of burning candles and incense. It was quiet inside the sanctuary except for a few muffled coughs and whimpers from babies in the back. Then Father O'Brien crossed himself in front of the altar and began preaching.

I thought he'd never stop. He went on and on about the twins' spiritual maturity. Maybe he would have shortened that sermon if he'd known Violeta and Rosita the way I did. I couldn't sit still because the stiff collar of my tuxedo was choking me. Papá looked uncomfortable, too, and smiled at me sympathetically. I looked at the stained glass windows covered with saints, then at the statue of Jesus on the cross. If he could endure that suffering, I thought, I can put up with this tuxedo for a few hours.

The religious services finally ended with the priest presenting each twin with a Bible.

After church, we paraded through town like a wedding procession. My family and I rode in my uncle's car which was covered with white streamers. Everyone followed us to the American Legion Hall, the place Papá had rented for the reception.

The long, brick building was decorated inside

with pink balloons and white ribbons. A band wearing black suits sat on stage at the far end of the auditorium. It played soft music, the kind that made me sleepy. But most of the time I couldn't hear the musicians because of the fifty guests chattering in Spanish.

Everyone got quiet when the ceremony began. My parents marched into the center of the room, followed by the twins' godparents who happened to be our uncle and aunt. Next came the two birthday girls and their escorts.

I'd never seen my sisters look so beautiful. They wore lipstick for the first time and white, lacy dresses that almost touched the floor. The crowns on their heads and matching earrings, a gift from their godparents, sparkled. "Violeta and Rosita look like two Cinderellas," I whispered to a cousin standing next to me.

He grinned. "At midnight we'll see them in rags."

I choked back a giggle.

Thirteen other couples filed in as their names were announced. Counting the twins with their escorts, that made fifteen, the age of the birthday girls. The señoritas, all dressed in white, lined up on one side with their escorts in black tuxedos facing them.

Then everyone moved away, leaving only the twins sitting in folding chairs at the center of the floor. Kneeling down, Papá exchanged their flats for white, high-heeled shoes to show that the girls had become women.

In another part of the ceremony, each of the twins presented Marikita with a doll. This showed that they were no longer children. "Gracias," Marikita said, cradling a doll in each arm as though they were real babies.

Later, she stood between her sisters, holding hands with them while a man from the newspaper took their picture.

After scribbling down the names of the twins, he asked me, "Who was that little angel in the middle?"

"Marikita Díaz," I said. "She's la menor, the youngest of our family."

With Violeta and Rosita sitting in the center of the auditorium, my uncle made a speech about how wonderful they were. Then, turning to his two nieces, he said, "I present you to this society. Congratulations on your quince años."

Everyone stood and sang "Las Mañanitas," the birthday song.

After that, the band played a waltz. My father danced first with Violeta, who was five minutes older, then with Rosita. Next, all of the señoritas waltzed with their escorts. Finally everyone joined in the dancing.

I danced first with my cousin, Marta, who was two feet taller than I was and smelled like a perfume factory. I must have stepped on her feet a few times because she left me standing on the dance floor. "I'm going to put bandages on my toes," she said.

Then my brave little sister, Marikita, danced with me. The light radiating from her white, lacy dress reminded me of what the photographer had said. "Are you really a little angel?" I asked Marikita.

"Yes, I am," she said, beaming like she always did when she gave a correct answer in English.

The wonderful aroma of carne asada, broiled beef, drifted across the room. Everyone sat at the long tables, eating. Every few minutes someone raised a glass of champagne in a toast to Violeta and Rosita.

After dinner, people stood around drinking more wine. I walked among the guests with a glass of lemonade, pretending that it was champagne.

The best thing, though, was the birthday cake which stood almost as tall as Marikita. It had fifteen candles and thick, white icing. The twins cut it and each ate a piece before my aunts served it to the guests. I had two helpings.

The party began to break up at midnight when the band left. We were all tired but happy, especially the twins who got a car load of presents. As we left the building, some boys from my class rode their bicycles through the parking lot. Seeing me, Owl stopped. I started to walk over to him, but Papá said, "Get into the car, Jose."

Chapter XVII
JOSE, CAN YOU SEE THE TURKEY?

By late November, the days had grown cold, and the smell of wood smoke filled the air. All of the trees except the live oaks had turned brown or yellow. Early in the morning the grass was covered with frost and crunched beneath my feet as I walked to school.

To avoid going by Owl's house I cut through Mr. Gibson's field, where shocks of hay stood in rows like tepees in an Indian Village. At the edge of Oak Grove I crossed the highway at Johnson's Market, which had pyramids of pumpkins along the outside wall. I turned on Main and followed it past the elementary school where drawings of Indians and pilgrims decorated the windows.

I used to hate Thanksgiving because it reminded me that I was different. In fourth grade, Gerald asked, "Why do you celebrate Thanksgiving, Jose? Your ancestors didn't come to America on the Mayflower."

"No, they came on the Santa María with Columbus," I said.

T-Rex grinned. "I thought they swam the Río Grande."

Everyone laughed, and my faced burned with embarrassment. But what he said wasn't too far from the truth. My family arrived here as migrant workers and stayed because Papá got hired at the refinery. If he lost his job there, we'd probably have to go back to Mexico. None of us wanted that except, maybe, Mamá.

This year in junior high, we kids didn't do the Thanksgiving stuff we did in elementary, such as drawing around our fingers to make a turkey. For the first time I can remember we didn't do that silly play about Indians and pilgrims eating a feast together in 1621. I hoped we weren't going to have any work about Thanksgiving. But in Language Arts, Miss Rose made us write a short dialogue that might have taken place between the Pilgrims and the Indians.

In mine, Chief Wampanoag asked William Bradford, "How long are you people going to stay in our country?"

"Oh, just a few thousand years," replied the governor.

Everyone laughed except T-Rex and Owl who just sneered.

Like always, we had our Thanksgiving lunch at school on Wednesday. Mamá let me buy because she knew how much I liked turkey. That was something we almost never got at home. Everything they served in the school cafeteria tasted good except the cranberries. Ugh! I didn't eat many of them.

For most kids the best thing about Thanksgiving was being out of school for the four day weekend. But staying home wasn't a lot of fun for me. I woke up that Thursday morning feeling lonely. Owl wouldn't be coming over, and my cousins had returned to Mexico.

Without knocking, Marikita swung open the door and hopped into my room, gobbling like a turkey. "Jose, you make a Mayflower for me?"

"Sure, Mija," I said.

After breakfast, I stayed at the kitchen table and sketched the ship on a blank sheet of notebook paper. I thought it looked pretty good with its tall sails and flag of England. "Come here, Marikita, and help me color it."

She took one look and frowned. "Un barco no es una flor."

I explained that the Mayflower really was a

boat, but she wouldn't believe me. Finally I just drew a sunflower like the ones on the table cloth. "That's right," she said, coloring it a bright yellow.

Papá slept until noon. Then we gathered at the kitchen table. "This is Turkey Day," I said right after our prayers. "That's what the kids at school call it."

"Why can't we have turkey?" asked Rosita. "Everyone in America eats turkey on Thanksgiving Day except us."

"You know how much your father hates turkey," said Mamá.

"It's not 'el día de pavo,' turkey day," he said. "It's 'el día de gracias,' a day to be thankful. And I'm thankful that we're not eating turkey." After filling his plate, Papá started the enchiladas around the table.

Everyone took a generous helping except Marikita. "I don't like enchiladas," she said, crossing her arms. "I want turkey."

Mamá whispered something in her ear, and my little sister smiled.

"I wish Ricardo was here to eat with us," she said. "Why doesn't he come anymore?"

We all waited for someone to answer. Finally Mamá said, "Right now Ricardo and your brother aren't getting along very well."

"This is the first Thanksgiving he hasn't spent the whole day with us," said Violeta.

"That's another reason to be thankful," mumbled Papá with his mouth full of enchilada.

"Papá, would you pass the turkey," I said after eating all the enchiladas on my plate.

He frowned. "Jose, can you see the turkey?"

"I can," said Marikita, pointing at the dish of enchiladas.

Everyone laughed except Papá who stopped eating and pulled at his mustache. But by the way his eyes twinkled we all knew that it was all right for Mamáa to hide the turkey in the enchiladas.

That was a wonderful día de gracias. We were thankful for the food and for being together as a family. But I still missed Owl.

Chapter XVIII
WHEN WILL COME THE WAR?

Our country was getting ready for war. Everyone knew it was coming except President Roosevelt. He said the United States wouldn't fight.

Military planes passed over Oak Grove almost every day, army trainers from San Antonio and navy aircraft out of Corpus Christi. At school, we watched them from the classroom windows and while we were outside at lunch time. We boys learned to identify biwinged Stearmans and monoplanes such as the Rayan PT22 and the Fairchild PT 19.

Best of all was when the war planes engaged in mock dog fights. They were so noisy our teachers had to quit talking until the pilots took their games somewhere else.

The airplanes were exciting but sometimes scary. About 3:30 Monday morning, I awoke to a loud roar. Jumping into my trousers, I charged into the kitchen.

Mamá and Papá came through the door, wearing pajamas and carrying a sleeping Marikita. They were followed by the twins in night gowns.

Everyone began talking at once. "Did you hear that?"

"What was it?"

Then we heard the thunder of aircraft flying low overhead. All of the windows in the house vibrated as a plane turned in tight circles. We ran outside to see what was happening.

The airplane dropped a flare which lit up the whole countryside. "It's Hitler," yelled Papá, pulling at his mustache. "He's come to bomb the refinery."

My heart jumped into my throat, and Marikita began sobbing. Mamá held her tightly, rubbing her back.

Papá hadn't meant to scare us with his silly joke, but Mamá yelled, "Why do you say things like that?"

Papá looked down, embarrassed.

Marikita rubbed her eyes and asked the same question that people all over America were asking. "When will come this war?"

At school, later that morning, I learned that the airplane had scared everyone in Oak Grove. "It was just an army air force trainer flying out of

Randolph Field in San Antonio," said Mr. Tuffit at an assembly of the whole school. "The pilot got lost and dropped a flare to see where he was."

That made us students feel a little better. But we all knew that America was getting more and more involved with World War II. People talked about it at home, at church, and at school.

In social studies we discussed the war every day and wrote papers about what was happening in Europe and the Orient. But a lot of times we just listened to Mr. Bradshaw. Pacing back and forth in front of the classroom, our thin gray-headed teacher told us about his experiences fighting in the trenches of France during World War I.

Margaret raised her hand. "It must have been terrible with all that killing and the poison gas."

He nodded. "But World War II is much worse. Thousands of people have already been killed in London and the other cities of Europe and China. Soon we'll be swept into this war just like we were in the other."

"Mr. Díaz," our teacher said, looking at me. He always called us by our last names. "What is isolationism?"

I thought for a minute. "It's the policy of the

United States to stay out of the war."

"Sort of," he agreed. "But since we're already helping our allies by giving them something to fight Germany and Japan with, we're not really neutral, are we?"

Mr. Bradshaw looked down at his roll book. "Miss Smith." The blond-headed girl in the front row scooted down in her desk. "What is lend-lease?"

Several hands shot up, but Mary smiled. "I know that one," she said, straightening herself up. "The United States is giving guns, airplanes, ships, and other supplies to Britain and Russia now. But those countries won't have to pay for them until after the war."

"Very good," said Mr. Bradshaw, nodding.

Before he could ask another question, the bell rang. But even in math we didn't escape the war. Mrs. Dozier gave us all kinds of story problems about the weight of battleships and the cost of military aircraft.

Tuesday, when the art teacher came, we did water coloring. While the girls painted houses and flowers, the boys sketched war planes. Most of us drew Spitfires, like those that had defeated the German Messerschmitts last year in the Battle of Britain. Robert brought a magazine picture of a Spitfire in a dogfight with a German warplane. He taped that photograph to the board so we could use it as a guide.

I outlined the British fighter with the tip of the brush, being careful to get in the details such as the four-bladed prop, the tail wheel, and the four machine guns on each wing. I added the red, white, and blue flag of Britain on its tail and used those same colors for the "bull's eye" circles on the side of the airplane, just behind the cockpit and on its wings.

"Look at Jose's," said Mrs. Miller, the red-headed teacher who taught us both art and music.

Several of the boys gathered around to admire my "masterpiece." But Owl and T-Rex sat over in the corner snickering.

Saturday it rained again. I worked on my theme assignment all morning. But when Papá woke up, I followed him into the kitchen where he sat down with a cup of coffee. "May I go to the matinee this afternoon?"

"I don't know." He twisted his mustache. "I'm saving money for those golf clubs."

Then, grinning, he dug into his pocket and flipped a dime to me. "That's for not getting into trouble this week."

It was the first time I went to the movies without Owl. I saw him sitting in the front row with T-Rex and his friends. They were throwing popcorn up and trying to catch it in their mouths. I figured that would be easy for the dinosaur.

I liked the main feature a lot. It was a western with Roy Rogers and his horse, Trigger. Following that came a short serial in which Buck Rogers crashed on Mars. With his rocket ship burning, he struggled to get the door open. Then, while all of us kids bit our fingernails, the narrator said, "Continued next week."

A lot of people left the theater when the "March of Time" newsreel started, but I stayed because it was about the war. The film showed the Japanese Zeros dropping bombs on the cities of China.

I remembered Mr. Bradshaw saying those war planes would attack the United States, too. I wondered if my teacher was only guessing. But everyone said that the United States would get into the war pretty soon.

As I started walking toward home after the movies, I glanced at the crooked tower and thought about Marikita's question. When will come this war?

Chapter XIX
WHO'LL HAUL THE OIL?

Oak Grove had its own little war over the strike. Papá said that even the strikers were fighting among themselves. Some of them wanted to join a union called the C.I.O. Others didn't because that would mean paying dues. But every day some of the men stood in front of the refinery waving their picket signs.

Mamá cried and begged Papá not to go to work because she thought the strikers might hurt him. But each afternoon he marched right through them, even though they called him bad names.

He wasn't the only one who refused to strike, though. There were enough workers to keep the refinery producing oil and diesel as long as they had crude oil to refine. But one night the transport drivers refused to cross the picket line.

When I carried my father his hot supper Friday night, I saw a big, shiny oil tanker parked crossways in the street so other trucks couldn't get into the refinery.

I sat with Papá in the tin hut by the boilers while he ate his tacos. Through a dirty window, I watched the two big steam pumps swishing back and forth. Shut down, shut down, they seemed to say. "Papá, will the refinery have to shut down now that it can't get any more crude oil to refine?"

"No, Mijo. Tomorrow the trains will start bringing in more crude oil. But tonight we'll do it."

He got up from his chair. "Are you staying here with me all night?"

I followed him out the door. "Sí. Mamá said I could come home with you in the morning. She thinks the strikers won't hurt you as long as I'm around." I flexed the muscles of my arm to show how strong I was.

Papá grinned.

Inside the little square office building, we found Robert Blake sitting at his desk. I'd seen him many times before, an older man with white whiskers and a wooden leg. He limped over and shook hands with me. "Hello there, Jose Jr. Did you come to haul oil?"

Papá smiled. "We're ready, Sir."

Mr. Blake nodded. "I'll keep an eye on the boilers, Jose. You just bring us something to refine."

After saying goodbye to the foreman, I followed Papá behind a row of oil tanks to a rusty truck. "When the refinery bought the new transports," Papá explained, "it kept the old ones for moving asphalt. But tonight we use them to haul crude oil."

Papá climbed inside the cab. He reached down and pulled me up, since my legs were too short to reach the running boards. The starter made a grinding noise, then the engine came to life with a roar. The seats vibrated so much I felt like I was riding in our Model A Ford with a flat tire.

After the air pressure gauge moved from red into the green, Papá drove the big rig out of the refinery along the back road. When we stopped at the railroad tracks, I got out and swung open the big metal gate. It squeaked as if it hadn't been used for a long time.

We crossed the wooden bridge over the Río Frío, then bounced down a dirt road that took us out of town. Sand swirled up through cracks in the cab's floor and felt gritty on my face. It got worse every time we met another truck. I couldn't see anything through the windshield except a wall of red dust that made me sneeze. "Papá, where's the road?" I asked.

"I don't know, Mijo," he said. "But I hope it's straight ahead."

Finally, we arrived at the refinery's oil lease and drove past a lot of steel derricks. They looked like ladders climbing up to the stars. Big, steel oil tanks also stood along the road. We stopped beside one. Papá connected a hose to it and started the truck's pump. Clank, clank, clank went the machine, shaking the floorboard as it sucked oil into the tanker.

Every few minutes, Papá climbed on top to see how full it was getting, then returned to the warm cab. I stared through the window at the pump jacks going up and down as they pulled the crude oil from deep inside the earth. "They look like giant grasshoppers," I said.

"Tú tienes una imaginación gigante," he said, laughing.

I guess I do have a giant imagination, I thought. I'll need it when I become a writer someday.

I liked everything about hauling oil except crossing that old, wooden bridge by the migrant workers' camp. There was no problem going over it empty as we left the refinery. But coming back onto that rickety bridge with a full load scared me spitless. As Papá inched the truck across in low gear, the timbers groaned and the railings shook. So did I when I looked down at the dark waters of the Río Frío far below. Each time we crossed, I wondered if the bridge would fall. But it was still standing when we reached the other side, so I began breathing again.

We worked on through the night until the sun turned the eastern sky pink. Jose, can you see by the dawn's early light? I thought.

No, I can't. I'm too sleepy to see.

I don't know how many loads of oil we hauled into the refinery. Mostly I napped until we came to the river crossing. No one could sleep through that.

When Papá stopped at the railroad gate, I opened it and watched for trains while he drove the tanker truck across the tracks. I didn't spot a single train that night.

Chapter XX
WHY DID IT HAPPEN?

December blew in with another norther, cold and wet. I walked to school in the rain and came home in the rain. But that evening, when Mamá asked me to take Papá his hot supper, I didn't want to go out in the wet weather again. "Why can't you just drive his dinner to him?" I asked.

She hesitated. "I don't drive so good at night," she said, but finally agreed to do it this once.

I was angry with Marikita for piling into the front seat by Mamá so that I had to sit in the back. Swish, swish went the wipers, trying to sweep the water off the windshield, but the whole world looked blurry.

At the refinery's parking lot many of the strikers sat in cars. Some of them had their families with them. Owl was sitting in the back seat of their Chevrolet with his window down. As we approached, my former friend tapped his father on the shoulder and said something to him. Then Mr. Krause got out of his car, carrying a sign. When Mamá tried to drive past, he stepped in front of our Model A. "I'm sorry, Mrs. Díaz," he said, "but nobody crosses this picket line."

"I know another way," I told her.

She drove across the rickety bridge and stopped at the back gate. When I swung it open, I didn't even think about trains. Mamá drove through, but the old Ford stalled on the tracks. I heard Mamá scream, then spotted the string of tank cars backing toward the Model A.

"Mamá!" I yelled, racing up the little hill.

The train hit on Marikita's side and pushed our car down the tracks about a hundred feet, before flipping it upside down into the ditch. Mamá was still inside, but Marikita lay beside it in the rain.

She felt so light when I picked her up, as if she wasn't really there. I carried her toward Papá who came running with some other men. Seeing the crumpled rag doll in my arms, he screamed, "NO! NO! NO! Not Marikita!"

Someone put Marikita and me in a car which raced through town with its horn blowing. I sat in the backseat, still holding my little sister.

Brushing the wet hair from her face, I whispered, "It'll be okay, Mija."

At the hospital, the doctors and nurses took Marikita from me and put her in another room. They kept trying to examine me because I was covered in blood. "Just leave me alone!" I yelled.

Papá and Mamá arrived in another car. Leaning against him, she staggered through the hospital door with a large bump on her forehead. After hugging me, she said, "Where's Marikita?"

I couldn't say anything. My tongue seemed to be stuck. But when Mamá saw the tears sliding down my face, she began to scream. "Dónde esta mi hija? – Where's my baby?" She screamed that over and over again until the doctor gave her a shot. Then they put her in another room where she could sleep. Papá stayed with her, holding her hand.

My little sister was gone, and I couldn't stand the emptiness in my life. I charged out the hospital door and down the street as fast as I could. Passing the houses and stores, I ran and ran and ran. Gasping for air, I staggered into the arms of a man waiting there on the sidewalk. Someone at the hospital must have called him.

Looking into his face, I saw it was Sheriff Madfellow. Only this time he wasn't mad. Tears flowed down his cheeks and mixed with the rain.

He drove me back to the hospital. Owl's mom had brought the twins. We hugged, then sat in the waiting room all night, crying until we had no more tears.

Staring out the window, I saw that the rain had changed to snow. Large flakes floated gently down like white leaves until the ground and trees lay beneath its whiteness. Marikita had never seen snow and never would. But I pictured her sitting here beside me, her eyes sparkling like the snow outside, and saying, "Qué bonita, Jose! Isn't it beautiful?"

It snowed more on the day of her funeral, like God was trying to cover up this terrible tragedy with tiny, sparkling diamonds.

At mass, the building was full. People were there I'd never seen at church. All my class sat in two long pews near the front, even Owl. I couldn't stand to look at him. Why are you crying? I thought. Marikita wasn't your sister!

Then I glared at the statue of Jesus hanging on the cross. Why, Lord? I asked him. Why did this happen to Marikita?

I don't remember anything Father O'Brien said, only that he wore a white robe as did the altar boys. I just sat there with my family, staring at Marikita's little white coffin with the candles burning near it. The smell of hot wax and incense filled the church.

When the priest finally stopped talking, we had another procession. As the line of cars followed the hearse slowly through town, people along the sidewalk watched respectfully. All the men took off their hats.

We arrived at the cemetery and stood facing the small coffin. Father O'Brien spoke some more words, but I didn't listen. Instead, I turned around and watched the people walking up the hill. It seemed the whole town had gathered here to say goodbye to Marikita, a little girl that many of them didn't even know. Most of the people stood in family groups. But Owl sat alone on the snowy ground where we'd had our discussion on Halloween. I wondered if he was thinking about bringing Marikita some candy next year on The Day of the Dead.

On the way home I could see the question mark at the refinery, poking into the gray sky. Why Marikita? I asked. Why? Why? echoed the steam pumps.

Chapter XXI
IT'S STILL A QUESTION MARK

Every night, I stared out my window at the crooked tower, sticking up into the dark sky. Decorated now with strings of colored lights, it looked like a Christmas tree. But I knew it was only the question mark, wearing a disguise.

A couple of weeks had passed since Marikita died. We all missed her a lot, even the hound, Feliz. Although I took food to him every day, he just lay in the hay, looking up at me with those sad eyes. Then, one day, when I went to the barn, he was gone. He must have decided it was too lonely here without Marikita.

Sometimes, when the twins were out, I went into their room to stare at Marikita's bed. The two quinceañera dolls sat there, looking beautiful in their white lacy dresses. I wished she could have taken them with her. Do little girls play with dolls in heaven? I wondered.

One night Mamá stood in the yard, looking

up at the stars. "They're the souls of little children," she said, "shining in the sky for the whole world to see."

I knew they were just suns so far away they looked small. But what Mamá said sounded right, too. Marikita had to be up there somewhere, watching us, loving us.

Every morning, I woke up crying and looked out my window at the question mark. Why did she die? Jose, can you see?

No, I can't.

A lot of us felt guilty about Marikita's death. I wished I'd just taken Papá's dinner to him when Mamá asked me to do it. She blamed herself for not learning to drive well. Papá said, "If I had gone on strike with the others, Marikita wouldn't have died."

Even Owl's father came to the door one morning, crying and begging Mamá to forgive him. "If I hadn't stopped you from going through the front entrance," he said, "your daughter would still be alive."

I couldn't believe it when Mamá hugged him.

Everyone was kind to us after the accident. People I didn't know left food on our doorstep. Rex brought some money collected at his father's church to help with the burial expenses.

Someone even put new tires on my bicycle. I figured Owl did that.

He knocked on the door one day. I didn't let him in, but he put a box of candy on the porch and a letter addressed to me.

I remembered him in the refinery parking lot that night, laughing when his father made us use the back gate where the train killed Marikita. I threw both his candy and the unopened letter into the trash.

Another bad thing happened after Marikita died. On Sunday, December 7, 1941, the war finally came. Japanese war planes bombed the United States naval base in Pearl Harbor, sinking a lot of our ships and killing thousands of Americans.

Two days later, my family gathered around the radio and listened to President Roosevelt. He announced that we were now at war with Japan and the other nations fighting against our country. Papá said, "This war will go on for a long time, and millions of people will be killed."

Worried that Papá might be drafted into the army, Mamá wanted us to move back to Mexico.

"No," Papá said. "If I'm called on to fight, I will. But people are saying the refinery workers must remain here to make oil and fuel for the war effort."

That was why some men from the government made the strikers go back to work.

All of this talk about the war was sad, but mostly I just missed Marikita.

I didn't want to go back to school, but Papá said that I had been out long enough. The twins had already returned to class.

At least my theme was almost finished. Miss Rose came over last week and read some of it. "Your ideas are wonderful," she said, smiling, "but some of your English sentences need fixing."

I corrected all the mistakes I could find.

While I was combing my hair that morning, I noticed that my eyes were still red from crying. The mirror which faced the window also reflected Owl walking onto the porch. For a long time he just stood there. Finally, he knocked.

Hoping that he'd go away, I didn't open the door. Later, when I looked out the window, he was still sitting on his bicycle, as though nothing had happened between us.

He'd even pushed my bike out of the garage and stood it next to his. The bright sunlight reflected off the handlebars.

Several times Owl glanced at his watch. It was

way past time for school, but still he waited.

You can wait there forever, I thought. I'm not coming out.

Then I remembered Marikita. Whenever Owl had knocked, she'd skipped across the room and swung open the door. With a smile on her face as cheerful as a sunflower, she grabbed his hand and led him into our home.

Marikita was gone now, but the memory of her love and sweetness still lived. If I wrote it down in a book, it would never die.

Jose, can you see?

I think so.

Slowly I opened the door and strolled over to Owl. He wouldn't look at me. He just kept kicking the ground with his tennis shoe.

"Hey, Ricardo," I said, "how far can you spit?"

Suddenly he dropped the bicycle, and we hugged, crying like two babies. After a little while, Mamá brought out a warm tortilla for each of us. We rode off for school eating them.

*

Printed in the United States
16030LVS00001B/143-194